A Translation and Appreciation

of

Selected Tang and Song Ci-poems

# A Translation and Appreciation

## of

# Selected Tang and Song Ci-poems

Lin Kong-hui

## 8 Dragons Publishing

1998 Hongkong

Published by 8 Dragons Publishing
5th Floor, 43 Maidstone Road, Kowloon, Hongkong

Distributed by Peace Book Co,Ltd.
Room 1502 Wing On House,
71 Des Voeux Road Central, Hongkong

© July 1998   Lin Kong-hui
ISBN   962-7328-33-2
Printed in Hongkong

文化交流是世界文明的歷史使命，而
詩是人類的靈魂。我希望這本書能成
爲東方的燕子。

林　庚*

Cultural exchange is the historical mission of
world civilization, while poems are the soul of
mankind. I hope this book will become an
eastern swallow flying in the western blue sky.

Lin Geng*

* Professor of Beijing University　北京大學教授

# 前　言

一九四五年秋，我到福建長汀讀廈門大學中文系。那時系主任是余謇先生（字仲詹），正爲高年級同學講「詞選及習作」課。我因爲是新生，尚閒着無事，便也前往旁聽。次年，廈大遷回廈門，仲詹師爲我班講課，曾向我極口稱讚上班女同學林孔輝的詞作，說是才、情兩勝。類似這樣誇她的話，我從別的老師處也多次聽見過。

一九四八年夏，林孔輝學長先我畢業後離校。一晃近四十年，我又有幸在南京會見她。此時，她已是南京郵電學院的英語教授了。去年十一月，我重經白下，聽說她的《唐宋詞英譯及鑒賞》已脫稿，很想先讀爲快。果真不久，當我從外地回來，便發現書桌上已放着她寄來的書稿了。她囑我作序。我雖不敏，但怎敢推辭呢？所以只好硬着頭皮寫幾句。

這本書選譯了唐宋詞四十五首，並用英語寫了賞析。從所選篇目可看出，著者對詞的本色是深有領悟的。她沒選那些晦澀、板滯、堆砌典故或形同猜謎一般的作品。這除了出於英譯效果的考慮外，也表明著者的審美情趣更偏重於天然和清新。正如她在前言中所說：她自幼喜愛詩，每每被詩的藝術魅力所深深感動。她願把這種崇高的藝術享受分給外國朋友。

林學長的鄉前輩嚴復先生說得好：「譯事三難，信、達、

# Foreword

I arrived in Chang Ting, Fujian in the autumn of 1945 and entered the Chinese Department of Amoy University majoring in Chinese. At that time, the head of the Chinese Department was Mr Yu Qian, styled Zhong Zhan. He was teaching "Selected Ci-poems and Exercises in Compositions" for senior students. I was a freshman, and our classes hadn't begun yet, so I visited the advanced class. The next year, when Amoy University moved back to Amoy, Mr Yu taught our grade. He praised Lin Kong-hui, a student one year senior to me, for her ci-poems. He said that she was gifted and expressive. I heard many praises similar to this from other teachers.

In the summer of 1948, Miss Lin graduated and left our university. Forty years passed like a flash, and I was lucky to meet her in Nanjing again. This time she was an English professor in the Institute of Posts and Telecom.

Last November when I went up North, I heard that her work "A Translation and Appreciation of Selected Tang and Song Ci-poems" was completed. I considered it a pleasure to be among the first to read them. Just as I expected when I returned home, I found her manuscript on my desk. She asked me to write an introduction. Though I am unworthy, how can I dare to refuse? So I braced myself and wrote these remarks.

This book contains forty-five selected ci-poems of the Tang and Song Dynasties, translated and appraised in English. From those chosen, we know that the writer comprehends deeply the true qualities of ci-poems. She did not select those that are obscure, dull, loaded with literary quotations, or riddle-guessing material. Besides considering the effect of the translation, she expressed that her temperament and

雅。」(《天演論·譯例言》)我限於英語水平，不敢妄吹她的譯詩已雅到何種程度。但譯文的信和達，那是粗通英語的人都能看出來的。

要做到譯文的信和達，也決非易事。許多著名的外國漢學家在翻譯中國古典詩詞時鬧笑話，那是常有的事。聞一多先生《英譯李太白詩》(見《唐詩雜論》)和呂叔湘先生《中詩英譯比錄》中就舉出過不少這種例子。而林孔輝學長的這部譯著則無論在譯文方面或鑒賞方面，都做到了準確、通達甚至精采的地步。因此我相信此書出版後，必將受到海內外廣大讀者的歡迎，並將證明我以上所說的話決非溢美之辭。

是爲序。

蔡　厚　示*
一九九七年三月寫於
福建社會科學院獨柳居

interest of aesthetic standards was partial to nature, pure and fresh. As she says in her preface: " I have liked to read poems since childhood. " and " Everytime I read them I was fascinated or deeply moved. They are boundless artistic treats to me. " She conceived the idea of introducing those ci-poems abroad. She wanted to expose foreign friends to the same artistic treats, and allow them to share our country's excellent cultural legacy.

Yen Fu has given us three guides to evaluating a translation: faithfulness, expressiveness and elegance. With my limited level of English, I cannot comment on the degree of elegance of the translations, but as to the expressiveness and faithfulness, I dare say that any reader who knows English a little can grasp her depth and accuracy.

It is not an easy job attaining the qualities of faithfulness and expressiveness. Many famous foreign sinologists have made foolish mistakes in translating Chinese classical poems. In Mr Wen Yi-duo's " An English Translation of Li Tai-bai's Poems " and Mr Lu Shu-xiang's " The Notes of the English Translation of Chinese Poems ", a lot of such examples are cited. Miss Lin's works, not only in translation but also in appreciation, have been accurate, expressive and even brilliant. So I believe when it is published, it will be well received by the masses throughout our country and abroad. Facts will prove that the praise I have given has not been excessive.

Thus I wrote this introduction.

Cai Hou-shi*
March 1997, Fujian

---

* Research fellow of the Fujian Academy of Social Sciences 福建社會科學院研究員

# 序 言

唐宋詞(包括五代)以其卓越的藝術成就,千百年來,一直閃爍着奪目的光輝。許多名篇膾炙人口,千古傳唱,至今仍然使人從中得到無窮無盡的藝術享受。我編譯此書,主要想將中國的寶貴藝術遺產,介紹國外,讓那裏的愛好者也能共同享受。

甚麼叫詞?詞的全名是「曲子詞」。「曲子」是在宴會上演唱的曲調,「詞」則是與這些曲調相諧和的唱詞。唐宋時,人們或簡稱其爲「曲子」,或簡稱其爲「詞」,並無一定不變的稱呼。由於這些「曲子」的唱法今已不傳,現在我們所能欣賞的,就只剩下文詞了。「曲子詞」今之所以通行省稱爲「詞」,其原因蓋在於此。

詞起源於隋,隋滅陳後,南方和北方、漢民族和少數民族、中國和外國交融而有此產物。詞雖起於隋,但隋詞卻未能保存下來。因此,我們論述詞的發展史,得從唐代説起。

甘肅敦煌莫高窟藏經石室中發現的「敦煌曲子詞」是唐代(兼有五代)的民間創作。反映的社會生活面相當廣闊。

現在最早的文人詞爲唐李白之作。其「菩薩蠻」,眾所周知。到中唐,張志和、韋應物、戴叔倫和白居易等繼起。張志和的

# Preface

Tang-Song (including the Five Dynasties) Ci-poems' remarkable literature achievements have been radiating with dazzling brightness thousands of years. Many well-known pieces have won universal praises on everybody's lips. Up to now they are still boundless artistic treats to men. I compiled and translated this book in order to introduce these ci-poems abroad and expose some foreign friends to the same artistic treats and share our country's excellent culture legacy to them.

What does a ci-poem mean?

Ci-poem's whole name is " Quzi Ci". Quzi is a tune which is sung on a banquet. Ci is the words of the song which harmonizes with the tune. In the period of Tang and Song Dynasties, a ci-poem was called a " quzi" or a " ci" for short. There was no definite address for it. The way of the singing was not handed down, so we were only able to enjoy the words later. That was the reason why quzi ci was called ci in later generations.

Ci-poems originated from Sui Dynasty. Sui destroyed Chen, unified the country. Musics and literatures of the Northern part and the Southern part of the country, the Han nationality and the minority nationalities, China and foreign countries blended with each other so ci-poems were produced.

Although they originated from Sui, they were not preserved. When we discuss the developing history of ci-poems, we should begin with Tang Dynasty.

In Gansu Dunhuang Shiku (the Dunhuang Cave) Dunhuang Quzi Ci was discovered. It was the creations among the people of Tang and the Five Dynasties. It reflected a wide range of social life.

「漁歌子」，風流千古。此後，填詞之風盛行。到晚唐，這一新型文學樣式可說基本成熟。這時期的代表作家是溫庭筠。他的藝術水準很高，詞主艷情，其作品有「溫飛卿集」等。

五代時期，北方戰禍頻仍，南方局勢較穩定。前後蜀和南唐，經濟、文化都較發達，而有西蜀、南唐兩大詞派的產生。

「西蜀派」也稱「花間派」。溫庭筠是其鼻祖。韋莊是其中成就最高的詞人。

「南唐詞派」代表作家主要是中主李璟，後主李煜和宰相馮延巳。後主詞是用血和淚寫成的，十分感人。因該派形成時，已是國運衰微，其風格淒清而少綺麗。

北宋時期，統治階層養妓成風，市民階層也要文化娛樂的享受，上下社會對聲歌有共同的需求，構成詞的極盛時代。

藝術高峰出現在第三代君主仁宗時期。代表人物是晏殊和歐陽修。詞調以小令為主；詞風近似南唐馮延巳，藝術造詣很高。晏殊幼子晏幾道，善長小令，與乃父並稱「二晏」。市民詞代表人物是柳永，他精通音律，與民間樂工合作，創制了許多新腔。其中大多數是長調，打開了寫作長詞的道路。以上晏，歐，柳皆是婉約派的主要作家。

北宋建國六十年後，社會中的階級矛盾、民族矛盾和政治派別

The earliest scholar ci-poems preserved now were Tang Li Bai's works. His "Devalike Barbarian" was well known. Till middle Tang, Zhang Zhi-he, Wei Ying-wu, Dai Shu-lun and Bai Ju-yi succeeded. Zhang Zhi-he's "The Fisherman's Song" distinguished and admirable for ages. Many people wrote ci-poems since then. Up to Late Tang this new literature style was ripe basically. The ci-poet who could represent this period was Wen Ting-yun. His artistic level was very high. His ci-poems were bright-coloured and beautiful, romantic, gentle and lovely. His works have "A Collection of Wen Fei-qing" etc.

In the Five Dynasties, flames of war occured frequently in the northern part of the country. But the southern part was rather stable. The economy and culture of Qian and Hou Shu and the Southern Tang were comparatively flourishing, so Western Shu and Southern Tang schools, the two great ci-poems schools were produced.

The Western Shu school was also called "Between Flowers school". They compiled "A Collection Between Flowers". Wen Ting-yun was their earliest ancestor. Wei Zhuang was the most accomplished ci-poet.

Zhong Zhu Li Jing, Huo Zhu Li Yu and the prime minister Feng Yan-si of Southern Tang Dynasty were the most important ci-poets in Southern Tang school. The ci-poems of Hou Zhu were very touching, which were written by blood and tears. Because it was the time of decline and fall of the Southern Tang, the style of the ci-poems was lonely and sad, not gorgeous.

When Northern Song dominated the country, the ruling class kept a large number of prostitutes. The town people needed also the enjoyment of cultural recreation. Upper and lower societies both loved singing and dancing. The golden age of ci-poetry thus came.

The highest peak of art appeared in the period of Song Ren Zong. Yan Shu and Ou-yang Xiu were the representative figures. Their ci-style are similar to that of Feng Yan-si. Their artistic attainment

的矛盾尖銳化，因此，仁宗慶曆年間有「新政」，神宗熙寧、元豐間有「變法」。它們對社會生活各個方面影響很大，宋詞的「豪放派」因而興起。范仲淹曾抗擊西夏，主持「慶曆新政」，他的詞頗多新意，是詞壇的一聲雷鳴。北宋後期，王安石在詞中懷古詠史，爲「豪放派」立下創作綱領。蘇軾認爲詞「無意不可入，無事不可言」，他是豪放派的奠基人。蘇軾的學生對他的作風有不同的反響。如黃庭堅是暗中仿效；而秦觀表面上不便指摘，卻走自己婉約之路。

北宋晚期，婉約派的主要作家有周邦彥。無論是他獨立創作或在他領導下整理和創作歌曲，都具有嚴格的規範性。他制樂，音聲繁複多變，章法變法也極其能事。北宋末，金人南侵。凡具有正義感的詞人，無不高歌抗戰、北伐。「豪放派」盛行。代表作家有李綱和岳飛，岳飛的「滿江紅」是時代的最強音，它鼓舞着世世代代的子孫奮勇前進。

南宋的陸游和辛棄疾都是著名的愛國詞人。辛解放詞體，「以文爲詞」。從此，散文詞法，侵入了詞的領地。

南宋前期「婉約派」還有一位出類拔萃的女詞人李清照。她的藝術造詣很高，能用「淺俗之語發清新之思」。

姜夔和吳文英，各自創制不少新腔，使「婉約派」詞有中興景象。

was very high. Yan Ji-dao, the youngest son of Yan Su, was good at xiao ling (short ci-poems, about 10-60 charactors). He and his father were called "Two Yans".

The representative figure of town people ci-poems at that time was Liu Yong. He had a good command of temperament. He cooperated with folk musicians and created many new tunes. Many of them were long tunes (about 100-200 words). He opened the road of long ci-poems.

Liu Yong, Two Yans and Ou-yang Xiu all belonged to the camp of graceful and restrained school.

After the founding of the state for sixty years, the class contradiction, nationalities contradiction and factional strife in politics of the Northern Song became more acute. Between the years of Ren Zong Qing Li, there was "New Policy". During the years between Xi Ning and Yuan Feng of Shen Zong, there were "Political Reform". Those political events exerted a tremendous influence to every respect of social life." The bold and unconstrained school " of Song ci-poems was produced.

Fan Zhong-yan resisted the aggressors, Western Xia and took charge of "New policy of Qing Li". His ci-poems possessed considerable new meanings, belonged to this school.

Up to the later stage of Northern Song, Wang An-shi discussed politics and meditated on the past and praised the history events in his ci-poems. He set up the creation programme for " the bold and unconstrained school. Su Shi thought that " No meaning cannot be written into the ci-poem, no things cannot be discussed within them". He was the founder of the bold and unconstrained school.

Su Shi's students had different echo in his style. Huang Ting-jian followed the example of his teacher secretly. Qin Guan did not agree with Su Shi. He took his own way of graceful and restrained school.

陳人傑、文天祥是豪放派著名作家。

以上，對唐宋詞主要流派及代表作家做了簡單介紹。主要作家
的作品，本書均有選譯。但因篇幅所限，並非所有代表作品均
有介紹，特別是早已譯成英文的作品，因讀者在別處已見過，
便不選入。

詩與詞有何不同？

詩的形式為大家所熟悉，因此，在這裏只略談一二。詩經是四
言詩。到漢朝以後，就盛行五言詩。當時四言，五言皆可作，
詩的長短也無硬性規定。到唐朝，詩可分為古風和近體兩種。
唐以前的詩體，統稱古風，當時創造的新詩就是近體詩。近體
詩分絕句和律詩。絕句是四句的詩，每句有五言，也有七言，
律詩是八句的詩，有五言，也有七言。句子都講究平仄聲調配
和押韻。律詩中間的四句且要對仗，就是中間兩對句子，每個
字詞性要相同，一句中用了名詞，另一句也得用名詞；動詞，
都動詞。

詞在形式上與詩不同。音樂的要求更高。每首詞都有個調。字
數和行數是固定的。調都有名，叫詞牌。中國字都有四聲。第
一聲，用「－」符號表示，又稱平聲。第二、第三、第四聲用
「ˊˇˋ」符號表示，又稱仄聲。字該用平聲還是仄聲，那些句
子要押韻，都是固定的。因此每個詞牌代表的調，可用圖來表
示。以本書的第一首詞《菩薩蠻》為例：

Chou Bang-yan was an important ci-poet of graceful and restrained school in the later period of Northern Song. Not only his own creation but also under the leadership of himself, the arrangement and creation of the ci-poems of his students were all strictly standard, the sound was complicated and always changing.

Towards the end of Northern Song, Jin Ren committed aggression to the south. Those who possessed the sense of justice, all stood for war of resistance against aggression and Northern expedition. Ci-poems of the bold and unconstrained school were prevalent. The representative figures were Li Gang and Yue Fei. Yue Fei's " Man Jiang Hong" was the strongest sound of that time, which encouraged the coming generations advancing bravely.

Lu You and Xin Qi-ji were also famouse patriotic ci-poems. Xin Qi-ji liberated the style of ci-poems. Since then, proses entered ci-poems.

Another famous ci-poet of graceful and restrained school was Li Qing-zhao. She could use simple and plain words to express pure and fresh thought.

Later, there were Jiang Kui and Wu Wen-yin, who belonged to the graceful and restrained school, created many new tunes.

Chen Ren-jie and Wen Tian-xiang belonged to the bold and unconstrained school

We have introduced briefly the chief schools and the main representative writers of Tang and Song ci-poems. In this book we have selected their main ci-poems. Because of the limited space, we can't display all the representative works. Especially those which had been translated into English and the readers were already familiar with them.

What is the difference between poems and ci-poems?

I think the form of a poem you know very well. Here we'll just

◑○◑●○○●七字仄韻起

●○◑●○○●七字叶

◑●●○○五字換平韻

◑○◑●○五字叶


◑○○●●五字更仄韻

◑●○○●五字叶

◑●●○○五字更平韻

◑○◑●○五字叶

以上圖代表詞牌是「菩薩蠻」的調。○代表平聲，●為仄聲。
譜上為平聲而也可用仄聲，用◑。譜上為仄聲也可用平聲，用
◑。這首詞前段四句，兩句押仄聲韻，兩句押平聲韻。後段四
句，更換為兩句仄聲韻，兩句平聲韻。一共四十四個字，八個
韻。你若選這個調，就得按這個譜填。兩人都選這譜，兩首詞
都「調寄菩薩蠻」。本書雖未畫此圖，每首詞都有調名，每個
字都有四聲。可平可仄字上有⊙符號。平聲韻上有○，仄聲韻
上有●，與此圖意思相同。

寫此書時，得廈大校友們的熱情鼓勵和幫助。三位美國朋友
Professor Jan Engsberg, Professor Judy Caprowl 和 Dr. Sheppard 還為
我做了校對。在此，我表示衷心的感謝。

林孔輝

一九九七年五月

give a general review of them. The verse of the Book of Songs was four characters. Till Han Dynasty, the verse developed to five characters. But four or five characters both could be written. How long should a poem be? They did not lay down any hard and fast rule. In Tang Dynasty, the poems were divided into ancient customs and modern style poetry. Before Tang Dynasty. the style of a poem was called ancient customs. Modern style poetry referred to inovations in classical poetry. They have Jue Ju and Lu Shi. Jue Ju is a poem of four lines, each containing five or seven characters with a strict tonal pattern and rhyme scheme. Lu Shi is a poem of eight line, each containing five or seven characters with a strict tonal pattern and rhyme scheme .The middle four lines required duizhang, that is, the matching of both sound and sense in two lines usually with the matching words in the same part of speech.

The form of a ci-poem is not the same as a shi-poem and its music requirement is higher.

Poems written to certain tunes with strict tonal patterns and rhyme schemes, in fixed numbers of lines and words, is called ci-poem.

Chinese characters have four tones. The first tone, delimited by symbol ( — ) is also called level tone. The second, third and fourth tone, delimited by symbol " ✔ ∨ ❮ " and are also called oblique tone, because the fourth tone may replace the second and third tone.

Since every ci-poem has a certain tune with strict tonal pattern and rhyme schemes, every Chinese character has its own tone, we can use a graph to describe the ci-poem.Take Deva-like Barbarian, the first ci-poem of this book as an example:

◗○◑●○○●rhyme oblique
◗○◑●○○●rhyme oblique
◑●●○○rhyme level
◑○◑●○rhyme level

◑○○●●rhyme oblique
◐●○○●rhyme oblique
◑●●○○rhyme level
◑○◐●○rhyme level

The name of this tune is Deva-like Barbarian. It is composed of eight lines. Every line has its fixed number of characters. They are 7755, 5555. The numbers of the characters can't be changed. The tone of each character is also fixed. Symbol ○ represents level tone, symbol ● represents oblique tone, ◑ represents level tone in the table which can be changed into oblique tone. ◐ represents the oblique tone in the table, which can be changed into level tone, In the first part of this ci-poem, there are four lines. Two lines rhyme oblique, two lines rhyme level. In the second part of this ci-poem, there are also four lines. Two lines rhyme oblique, two lines rhyme level.

If you choose Deva-like Barbarian and fill the ci-poem, you should follow this rule. If your friend also fill this tune, both your ci-poems are called Deva-like Barbarian. It means you both use the same tune.

In this book we did not give you graphs like this one, but we gave you the names of the tunes, the tone of each character, the rhyme of every line. Symbol ○ means, " rhyme level", and symbol ⊙ means " rhyme oblique" symbol ⊙ means the word can be used as a level or oblique tone. These symbols express the same meaning as this graph.

When I wrote this book, my old teachers and friends in Amoy University encouraged me and gave me a lot of help. Three foreign teachers have also given me editorial assistance: Professor Jan Engsberg, Professor Judy Caprowl and Dr. Sheppard. Here I am very grateful to all of them.

Lin Kong-hui
May 1997

# Contents

XX

# A Translation and Appreciation

## of

# Selected Tang and Song Ci-poems

# Pú Sa Mán
# 菩薩蠻 **

## Dūnhuáng Qǔzǐ Cí
## 敦 煌 曲子詞 *

Zhěn qián fā jǐn qiān bān yuàn
枕 前 發盡 千 般 願，

yào xiū qiě dài qīng shān làn
要 休 且 待 青 山 爛。

Shuǐmiàn shàng chèng chúi fū
水 面 (上) *** 秤 錘 浮，

zhí dài huáng hé chè dǐ kū
(直待) 黃 河 徹底 枯。

Bái rì cēn chén xiàn
白 日 參 辰 現，

běi dǒu huí nán miàn
北 斗 回 南 面。

Xiū jí wèi néng xiū
休 即 未 能 休，

qiě daī sān gēng jiàn rì tóu
(且 待) 三 更 見 日 頭。

# Deva-like Barbarian

Anonymous

Before the pillow I vowed,
As far as I can, thousand oaths.
Wait,
Until the Green mountain rots,
On the surface of the water,
The sliding weight of a steelyard * * * floats,
The Yellow River thoroughly dries up,
I'll not fail to love you.

Unless
At daytime the Cen and Chen manifest themselves,
The Big Dipper returns to the south,
I'll not divorce you, but still it can't be done,
Till in the dead of night the sun rises.

---

* Dunhuang Quzi Ci was a large number of Tang and the Five Dynasties ci poems, discovered in the Dunhuang Caves, Gansu Province in 1900.
* * Explanation of symbols

Ci-poetry: Poems written to certain tunes with strict tonal patterns and rhyme schemes, in fixed numbers of lines and words, is called ci-poem. It is originated in the Tang Dynasty (618-907) and fully developed in the Song Dynasty (960-1279). Take this ci-poem as an example:

# Appreciation

When the sparks of love kindle two young hearts, the whole world seems to exist because of their joy. They treasure youth, longing for happiness. In the universe, they hope that their love will be eternal. So the sun, the moon and stars, rivers and mountains all become the incarnation of their feelings.

This ci-poem is a statement of a sweetheart to his/her beloved. In order to express his/her faithfulness, he/she swore passionate oaths as fire towards his/her lover. These oaths are formed by a series of most wonderful metaphors. They are highly creative.

The first sentence: "Before the pillow I vowed, as far as I can, a thousand oaths." points out the subject. "Vowed as far as I can" are very powerful words which show the thorough sincerity of the hero/ heroine at the happiest time. The lovers earnestly hope that they would be intimate with each other forever. So he/she cites

---

The name of this tune is "Deva-like Barbarian." It is composed of eight lines. Every line has its fixed numbers of words. They are 7755, 5555. The numbers of words can't be changed, the tone of each word is also fixed. The last word of every line rhymes. Chinese characters have four tones. The first tone (-) is also called level tone, the second (ˊ)、third (ˇ) and fourth tone (ˋ) are also called oblique tone. It is because the fourth tone may replace the second and third tone. In the patterns each word has its own tone, either level tone or oblique tone, some words either will do, which is also fixed as in this ci-poem. Symbol ⊙ means the word can be used as a level or oblique tone. Symbol ● means a rhyme of the oblique tone. Symbol ○ means a rhyme of level tone. The symbols are put above the words to show their tones. We have given every name of the tune its rule in this book. You can find them in each ci-poem. If you are interested in writing a ci-poem, you can follow this rule to fill one. It is the reason why we do not say writing a ci-poem but say filling a ci-poem.
＊ ＊ ＊ This was a folk ci-poem of its early stage, which form was still not fixed. It has Chenzi, that is , word inserted in a line of a ci-poem for balance or euphony, such as : "shang" (上), "zhi dai" (直待) and "qie dai" (且待) in this ci-poem, (we put brackets on them to show the difference), are all Chenzi.
A Chinese steelyard is made of a scaled lever and an iron sliding weight. Its effect is just like a balance scale.

three instances in which it would be impossible to imagine what he/ she firmly believes the tragedy of their love would happen. The first and third metaphors place the meaning on mountain and river. In the mind of ancients moutains and rivers were all symbols of the eternal. Since " the green mountain rots " is an out-and-out fabrication, their love would never change indeed. At the same time, that the Yellow River might thoroughly dry up is absolutely impossible too. What is called " wait, until " is in no position to begin. The second metaphor is taken from daily life which is appropriate and vivid. The sliding weight of a steelyard is often made of iron. As a proverb says: " Though a sliding weight of a steelyard is small, it can weigh a thousand jin. " Iron is heavy and it is much heavier than water. The sliding weight of a steelyard will never float on the surface of water, of course. The second part follows the first one closely. The hero/ heroine takes vows in succession. What is different is the hero/ heroine adopts metaphors from heaven instead of earth. The two stars, Cen and Chen, never exist simultaneously. As one falls, another rises. How can they both appear in the daytime? In the dead of night, the curtain of darkness is thick, and if the sun rises, is it contrary to reason? Day and night are in motion, which is the law of nature. The imagination of the hero/ heroine is only a desire that stresses the everlasting and unchanging nature of their love. The Big Dipper is always in the north. " Returns to the south " are also words expressing an impossibility. The hero/heroine cited six things at one go, so true, so sincere, one can well perceive his/her unreasoning passion. This ci-poem is permeated with intense emotion. It is very touching. In art , the greatest characteristic of this ci-poem is that it is good at using metaphors. " The green mountain rots ", " the sliding weight of a steelyard floats ", " the Yellow River dries up ",

" the Cen and Chen manifest themselves in the daytime ", " the Big Dipper returns to the south " and " the sun rises in the dead of night " are all metaphors. The author repeatedly stresses the impossibility, accomplishes them without any interruption, just like a summer storm, suddenly appears and suddenly stops in order to express his/her turbulent inner world. The writing is overflowing with enthusiasm, full of strength.

# Pú Sā Mán
# 菩薩蠻

Lǐ Bái
李白

Píng Lín mò mò yān rú zhí
平林漠漠烟如織，
hán shān yī dài shāng xīn bì
寒山一帶傷心碧。
Mǐng sè rù gāo lóu
暝色入高樓，
yǒu rén lóu shàng chóu
有人樓上愁。

Yù jiē kōng zhù lì
玉階空佇立，
sù niǎo guī fēi jí
宿鳥歸飛急。
Hé chù shì guī chéng
何處是歸程？
Cháng tíng lián* duǎn tíng
長亭連短亭。*

# Deva-like Barbarian

by Li Bai


The well-laid out woods are misty,
Vapours and smoke weave a screen,
Cold mountains stretch,
Which show a sorrowful green.
Dusk has fallen onto the tall buildings.
Someone is worrying upstairs.

She stands lonely,
On jade carved stairs.
Birds lodging for night,
Swiftly fly backwards.
Where is her dear one's way home?
Long pavilions succeed short ones.

---

* This word (連) ought to be the first tone or the fourth tone instead of the first tone, according to ci-poem's rule.

In ancient China, there are a lot of pavillions built along the road for travellers to take a rest. After ten li (里) there is usually a long pavillion, and five li, a short one.

# Appreciation

This ci-poem portrays a traveller staying long in a strange place and thinking of his lover. It has two parts. The first one has partiality for scenery depiction and the second stresses psychological description. In depicting the scenery there is strong subjective colour, while the psychological description is mixed with objective scenery. So taken as a whole emotion and scenery, subject and object together form a coherent entity.

The poet selects a time of deepening dusk, clouds and mist in late autumn to draw the picture. " The well-laid out woods are misty, vapours and smoke weave a screen " transmits a disconsolate emotion. They play the role of shrouding the whole text.

The mist spreads. It can't be torn down and cut off. Even the distant dark green mountains express grief, which worries the poet. From the mountain far away, the poet can't help thinking of his wife, remote from him. She must also worry at this time upstairs and long for her husband's return. The word " worry " connects all the melancholy, and gloom together. At the same time, it is a natural transition to the next part forming a connecting link between the preceding and the following.

In the deep dusk, she stood before the stairs for a long time. Her feeling is merely lonesome, " empty " is also an inevitable result from the sketch of the first part. The subjective emotion is not isolated. It melts into the scenery immediately.

Then comes " Birds lodging for night swiftly fly backwards. " This sentence is executed very well. The poet uses " Birds lodging for night " and " She stands lonely " to form a sharp contrast. On the one hand, the poet describes " the birds which fly swiftly " to serve as a foil to the woman who is in dire straits and has no one to depend on. On the other hand, since the birds return swiftly, the heroine's heart is disturbed more acutely. Thus the whole mood fluctuates. Seeing the birds, the heroine at this time hopes her husband will return naturally to their own home. Thus she could struggle to escape the endless worrying feeling. But where is his way home? Only long pavilions succeed short ones, no real answer is forthcoming. What she really feels is still continually down and out, disconsolate and lonely. In the short ci-poem, there, crowded together, is all this scenery: woods, mists, cold mountains, tall buildings at dusk, birds lodging for the night, long pavilions and short pavilions. Using them to express her feeling, the poet shows great skill. He develops the rich and complex world in her heart, reflecting the objective reality that he couldn't find his way home, giving readers a very disconsolate, gloomy mood. So we are deeply moved.

## A Brief Account of the Author's Life

Li Bai(701 — 762) styled himself Taibai. His old home was West Long(Gansu Province), Cheng Ji. His ancestors were banished to the Western Regions, Sui Ye(Xinjiang Province). When he was five, his family moved from the Western Regions to Mian Zhow, Zhang Ming (Si Chuan Province, Jiang You county). He left his native land at twenty-five and roamed over Xiang, Han, Wu, Yue and other places. At the beginning of Tian Bao, the imperial edict instructed him to join the Imperial Academy. But he was not thought highly of. In the period of Zhi De, he was an aide on the staff of Prince Yong, who conspired against the royalty and was executed. Li Bai was involved in trouble. He was also arrested and sent to prison. In the next year (in 758) he was sent into exile to Ye Lang (Guizhou Province, Tong Zi county). In 759, he was remitted and remanded. He died of disease in 762.

Li Bai was a famous poet in the Tang Dynasty. His style of poetry was powerful, bold and unconstrained, which was the peak of poetry about romanticism in ancient China. His writings have been compiled in " A Collection of Poems of Li Tai-bai ".

This poem was written when he was about 25, roaming over Xiang, Han, Wu, Yue. At that time he had just married the granddaughter of the former Premier Xu Yu-shi. The lady in this ci-poem may be her.

# Yú Gē Zǐ
# 漁歌子*

Zhāng Zhì-hé
張　志和

Xī sài shān qián bái lù fēi
西塞山前白鷺飛，
táo huā líu shuǐ guì yú féi
桃花流水鱖魚肥。
Qīn rùo lì　　lù suō yī
青箬笠，綠蓑衣，
xíe fēng xì yǔ bù xū guī
斜風細雨不須歸。

# The Fisherman's Song

by Zhang Zhi-he

Before Xisai mountain,
White herons are flying,
Peach blossoms falling.
Into the water floating.
Mandarin fish are fat.
With blue bamboo hat,
And green straw rain cap,
Though in slant wind and drizzle,
The fisherman needn't go back.

---

\* This tune followed modern style poetry Qi-jue(that is a four-line poem with seven characters to a line and a strict tonal pattern and rhyme scheme). Besides rhyming level tone, it may be level or oblique tone at first word. But, the note of " The rules of ci-poems of Wan Shu" says: " Since Song Dynasty, all ci-poems of this tune followed ' Xi Sai ' style. Authors now should write in accordance with this ci-poem. "

# Appreciation

Zhang Zhi-he's "The fisherman's Song" is a very famous ci poem, handed down through the ages. It has five pieces. This one is superior to all the others, so it has been well preserved. Owing to this ci-poem, Zhang is crowned with eternal glory.

Zhang was a member of the Imperial Academy awaiting imperial edict, but was banished from the court, so he later lived in seclusion. He was good at song lyrics, painting and calligraphy, and playing the flute. He also knew how to derive rich nourishment from the masses. "The fisherman's song" is a ci-poem which makes use of a folk song. It is very pure and fresh, simple and unadorned.

The author was not a fisherman, but a man of letters who found sustenance in mist-covered waters, so in this ci-poem there is not only the pure and freshness of folk literature, but the high ranking taste of the ancient man of letters who did not seek fame and wealth. We can say that. "The fisherman's song" is a song of a scholar with a fisherman's style, a song of a scholar depending on the fisherman and realizing the wonderful land of mist-covered waters. It has the splendour of a simple coming from nature and gives the readers the beauty of simplicity and ease.

This ci-poem has only twenty seven words, yet describes mountains, water, white herons and fat fish, describes slant wind and drizzle also writes about the fisherman's life which is leisurely and carefree. Though the poet wrote about "the fisherman" he actually wrote of himself. Special surroundings are arranged for the fisherman to show a picture of the fisherman's song, south in the lower reaches of the Changjiang River. The poet expresses his feelings through poetry and imagery. Being the centre of the picture, the fisherman wears a blue bamboo hat and a green straw rain cap. Through playing up scenery vigorously, the poet expresses the fisherman's inner world, which is carefree and content. The white herons are flying, the water flowing, scraps of peach blossoms are floating on the spring river. Mandarin fish are fat, swimming here and there. All the scenery is so fresh, pretty, the fisherman, of course, is attracted by them, producing natural and simple interest. He will not leave this place strengthening his resolve: not to go back into the dark society. As the reader, this naturally arouse our sympathy.

## A Brief Account of the Author's Life

Zhang Zhi-he, called Gui Ling originally, styled himself Zi Tong. He was a native of Jin Hua (now in Zhejing Province). When he was born and died is not known. In Su Zong of the Tang Dynasty, he was a member of the Imperial Academy awaiting imperial edict. Afterwards he lived in seclusion in all corners of the country. He was known as a mist-covered waters fisherman. His work is called "Xuan Zhen Zi", which he also used as his alternative name.

# Tiáo Xiào Lìng
# 調　笑　令

Dài Shū-lún
戴　叔倫

Biān cǎo, biān cǎo
邊草　邊草，

Biān cǎo jìn lái bīng lǎo
邊草盡來兵老。

Shān nán shān běi xuě qíng
山南山北雪晴，

qiān lǐ wān lǐ yuè míng
千里萬里月明。

Míng yuè, míng yuè
明月　明月，

hú jiā yī shēng chóu jué
胡笳一聲愁絕。

# Song of Teasing

by Dai Shu-lun


White grass of the border,
White grass of the border,
When the grass withers,
We draftees will be older.
On South of the mountain and North of it,
Snow is shining.
Over a thousand and a million Li,
The moon is bright.
Bright moon! bright moon!
A sound of reed,
Suddenly Sends me,
Into the utmost grief!

# Appreciation

This is a ci-poem of draftees longing to return home. The beginning of this ci-poem says: " White grass of the border, White grass of the border, When the grass withers, We draftees will be older. " which is in a strong exclamatory mood. At first the grass of the border is the same as other grass, but more tough and tensile, loved by oxen and horses. In autumn it withers and becomes white. Between 750-760, the Tang Dynasty lacked national strength. The court had to station a large number of soldiers at the frontier. From day to day, year after year, the stationary life frittered away the draftees' youth. Nobody cared for them. Nobody came to replace them. In such an endless and hopeless situation, whenever the grass of the border grew, the draftees also grew hope of returning home. As the time passed, the hope begun to fade. At last all hope was dashed with the withering of the grass. The draftees found their lot was as tragic as the grass of the border. " On South of the mountain and North of it, Snow is shining, Over a thousand and a million li, the moon is bright. " These two sentences describe draftees' pain of longing for returning. After a heavy snow, the weather is fine. Everywhere is silver white, setting off the moon in the night, especially bright and clear. The draftees looking at the moon think of their native land, which is natural and normal. Though the author did not point it out clearly, he used a reverse sentence style : let the draftees' eyes search for the snow on the south and the north of the mountain, let their thought move with the moonlight to their homeland a thousand and a million li away. The scenery is beautiful, but the feeling is grief. These words oppose each other and yet complement each other. A depressed and constrained feeling longing for returning home can't be reconciled, which is experssed between the lines. Facing the moonlight and then thinking of the homeland is the gist of this ci-poem. The poet puts " the moon is bright " at the end of the middle two sentences so that he can repeat " bright moon, bright moon " two times according to the tune. Thus the draftees' feeling of longing to return home overflows between the lines. However, when the draftee lowers his head pondering his homeland, the sound of a reed instrument awakened him. This prolonged war did not end, garrisoning the frontiers is endless. How could they not be weighed down with anxiety? The poet describes draftees longing to return home using grass of the border and the brightmoon, and writes the draftees' misfortune, through the use of a reverse sentence style, these skills make the feeling and the scene of this ci-poem complement each other. It is really wonderful, and gives the readers a rich association.

## A Brief Account of the Author's Life

Dai Shu-lun(732-789) styled himself You Gong or Ci Gong. He was a native of Run Zhou, Jin Tan(now part of Jiangsu Province). He worked as the county chief of Dong Yang in the De Zong court. Later, he was promoted to the prefectural governor in Fu Zhou(now Fu Zhou city of Jiangxi Province). In 788, he became the prefectural governor of Rong Zhou(now Rong county of Guangxi Province). He died while in office.

# Yì Jiāngnán*
# 憶 江 南

Bái Ju-yì
白 居 易

Jiāngnán hǎo
江 南 好，

fēng jǐng jiù céng ān
風 景 舊 曾 諳。

Rì chū jiāng huā hóng shèng huǒ
日 出 江 花 紅 勝 火，

chūn lái jiāng shuǐ lù rú lán
春 來 江 水 綠 如 藍。

Néng bù yì Jiāngnān
能 不 憶 江 南？

# Recalling Jiangnan*

by Bai Ju-yi

Jiangnan is wonderful,
The scenery of the past, I have known all.
At sunrise, river flowers are redder than fire,
In spring, river water is as green as blue.
How can't I recall?
The beauties of the whole.

---

* Jiangnan refers to the south of Yangtze River, including the southern part of Jiangsu and An Hiu and the Northern part of Zhejiang.

# Appreciation

Bai Ju-yi worked as a prefectural governor in Hangzhou from 822 to 824. In 825, he was transfered to Suzhou. He returned to Luo Yang because of eye disease in 826.

Suzhou and Hangzhou all were famous counties in Jiangnan. They were picturesque. The people there were distinguished and admirable. These made a good impression on Bai Ju-yi. He often wrote poems to cherish the memory of those places. This ci-poem was written when he was 67. "Recalling Jiangnan" is a ci-poem describing spring scenery. The full text has five sentences. At the very beginning, the poet praises: "Jiangnan is wonderful". Because it is wonderful, he couldn't help recalling it. The second sentence says: "The scenery of the past, I have known all." It expresses that the beautiful scene is known not by hearsay but by experience. So his recalling is memorable. That is to say, he not only wrote that the scenery was wonderful but also pointed out that it was worth recalling. Then he used two sentences to write Jiangnan's beauty: "At sunrise river flowers are redder than fire. In spring, river water is as green as blue." From the two phrases "At sunrise and in spring" we can see at that time in Jiangnan, when spring came, a hundred flowers were in bloom, which was all brilliant red. When the sun rose, the red sun illuminated every corner of the land, the red flowers became more flourishing. Here, because of the same colour setting off by contrast, the brightness is heightened. In spring, the river water was green, the red sun shone on it. The sunlight flooded the seashore. The green waves appeared more clear. The poet related flowers and river to each other, different colours set each other off. Originally, river flowers were red, river water was green. Now the red is redder, redder than fire, the green is greener, as green as blue.

A good poem needs the character of music and painting. But what moves people most is the emotion. So a good poem not only needs good rhyme and beautiful painting, but needs deep feelings as well.

Bai Ju-yi took feeling as the root of a poem. Whenever he wrote poems he used the true feelings to tug at others heart strings. This ci-poem is the fruit of his literature experience. Just as the title of this ci-poem, the whole text brims with the love of Jiangnan. Because the poet is deeply attached to it, he praises: " At sunrise river flowers are redder than fire, In spring, river water is as green as blue. " Here the writing of the scenery is just like a painting. But this is not only an objective scenery description but also the scenery of feeling created from deep emotion. Reading this ci-poem, we both see the beauty of Jiangnan and feel the poet's love of Jiangnan.

## A Brief Account of the Author's Life

Bai Ju-yi styled himself Le Tian. He was a native of Tai Yuan (now part of Shanxi Province). In 808, he was appointed Zuo Shi Yi, then banished to Jiang Zhou (now Jiangxi, Jiu Jiang) Si Ma. Later he was transfered to Zhong Zhou (now Zhong County in Sichuan Province) worked as a prefectural governor. Afterward he became the prefectural governor of Hangzhou, Suzhou and Tongzhou. He lived in Luo Yang at his later years. He used Mr Zui Yin and Xian Shan Lay Buddhist, as his alternative names.

Bai Ju-yi was a great realistic poet of Tang Dynasty and a poet who wrote more and better poems in the early stage of the Tang Dynasty. Some of his poems adopted the form of expression of folk literature. He had a certain influence on the development of the poetry of contemporary men of letters. His work has " A Collection of Mr Bai's Chang Qin Poems " . Now they are preserved in more than twenty pieces.

# Wàng Jiāngnán
# 望　江　南*

Wēn Tíng-yùn
溫　庭　筠

Shū xǐ bà
梳　洗　罷，

dú yǐ wàng jiāng lōu
獨　倚　望　江　樓。

Guò jìn qiān fán jiē bù shì
過　盡　千　帆　皆　不　是，

xié huī mò mò shuǐ yōu yōu
斜　暉　脈　脈　水　悠　悠，

cháng duàn bái pín zhōu
腸　斷　白　蘋　洲。

# Dreaming of Jiangnan

by Wen Ting-yun

Washing and dressing over,
I lean alone on the river watchtower.
A thousand sails all pass by thither,
No one carries my lover.
The slanting sunshine pulses on,
Green water floats along.
In Bai Pin Zhou,
My heart is broken.

---

* The name of this tune is also called " Recalling Jiangnan ".

# Appreciation

This ci-poem describes the melancholy mood of a woman longing for meeting her lover on a river watchtower all day long. The first sentence starts from "Washing and dressing" which points out the beginning of the time. Of course, it was early in the morning. The word "over" describes her eagerness to meet him. Just after she finished putting on her makeup she went to the river watchtower immediately. The second sentence puts its finger on the thing she looked forward to. "lean alone" excellently describes her mood. Because her worry was all by herself, she did not invite her girl-mate to accompany her and was not close to any one else either. "River watchtower" tells us the place where she stands and the object she longs for. In the river watchtower, one can only watch the river. On the river there are ships. So we know what she watches is the ships. "All pass by" tells us the process of her disappointment. In fact, this sentence contains her countless hopes and numerous disappointments. Whenever a ship came near, she perked up and looked at it closely. But none that passed by, carried her lover, she was disappointed. Under so many "no's", how deep was the distress she suffered? This sentence also expresses how long she has been standing. The last two sentences follows the third one closely which describes the feelings and mood after the heroine's disappointment. After sentences "A thousand sails all pass by thither, no one carries my lover", what appeared before her eyes was only "the slanting sunshine pulses on, green water floats along", and Jiang Zhou covered with white duck weeds. That means under the sunshine of the setting sun, all was silent. A boundless stretch of water flowed quietly. It hints that there was no hope that day. No ship would appear on the river. Only Jiang Zhou covered with white duck weeds was left. How sad would she be? she must be heart broken. The sentence "My heart is broken" tells us this strongly. They were not easily spoken.

# A Brief Account of the Author's Life

Wen Ting-yun (812 − 870) styled himself Fei Qin. He was a native of Tai Yuan in Shanxi Province. He was a gifted poet. Because of his talent he was swollen with pride. He often ridiculed influential officials. Besides, he lived a romantic life. So he was discriminated against by people in power. He was frustrated all his life, his social position was very low at that time. His poem in poetic world was called "Wen Li" (Wen, refers to Wen Ting-yun, Li, refers to Li Shang-yin, which means the poems of these two great poets enjoy equal popularity.) His achievement was less than Li's in shi-poetry, but his ci-poem opened up a ci-poetry style in its initial stage. In the development of ci-poetry history he has got an important position. His ci-poem was very elegant and gorgeous. Though most of their contents were maiden's complaint, their technique of expression was always changing its way, showing his excellent artistic attainments and exerting a profound and lasting influence on later generations.

# Pú Sà Mán
# 菩薩蠻

## Wēn Tíng-yùn
## 溫 庭 筠

Xiǎo shān chóng dié jīn míng miè
小 山 重 疊 金 明 滅，

bīn yún yù dù xiāng sāi xuě
鬢 雲 欲 度 香 腮 雪。

lǎn qǐ huà é mei
懶 起 畫 蛾 眉，

nòng zhuāng shū xǐ shí
弄 妝 梳 洗 遲。

Zhào huā qián hòu jìng
照 花 前 後 鏡，

huā miàn jiāo xiāng yìng
花 面 交 相 映，

xīn tiè xiū luó rū
新 帖 繡 羅 襦，

shuāng shuāng jīn zhè gū
雙 雙 金 鷓 鴣。

# Deva-like Barbarian

by Wen Ting-yun

Small hills are one on top of another,
On and off are their golden colour.
Cloud-like hair on my tempers,
Floats down to my cheeks as fragrant snow.
I got up idly, drawing my eyebrows,
Changing again and again,
I washed and dressed slow.

Looking at the front and back mirrors,
Across the shining face and petals,
Newly covered with embroiders,
The silk coat has a pair of golden partridges.

# Appreciation

This ci poem writes of a lady staying alone in her boudoir. She got up, made up and dressed herself. Through the description of all the activities in the morning, the poet showed her situation and mood.

The first two sentences describe the heroine's spirit of getting up. These two sentences are features, projecting the heroine's figure. The second one is the main body, the first one serves as a foil. " Small hills " is the picture on the bedstead, " golden " is the colour painted on them. " off and on " describes the sunshine through the window which shone upon the bedstead and made the light flash.

" Cloud-like hair on my tempers " describes the heroine's hair, black crimpy, lithe and graceful, like clouds. " Floats down " describes the hair swaying lightly as cloud floating. " to my cheeks as fragrant snow " writes of the heroine's face which is very fine and smooth, fresh and tender. All these stresses a delicate pretty lady's appearance. She just sits up on her bed. Her hair spreads out in a disorderly fashion which will float across her pretty face.

The third and fourth sentences describe her activity when she was getting out of a bed. " got up idly " reveals her mood. In the next sentence there is a word " slow ". These two words in particular show her listless mood.

The next part of this poem continues writing her activity. She looked at the mirrors, wore flowers on her head. " Across the shining face and petals " tells us that her face was as beautiful as the flowers. At this moment she enjoyed herself but had pity for herself too. She was so beautiful yet in the pinnacle of her youth, she was alone.

The last two sentences write what she wore after making up. Here the poet does not write of her activity but her eyes catching sight of her dress on which there was golden partridges in pairs, Just think, she had her heart filled with worry when she washed and dressed. Her spirit was very low originally. Now she saw the golden partridges in pairs, what would she think? This ci-poem's diction was ornate. Though a little hard to understand, if you read carefully, you will find it very charming.

# Gēng Lòu Zǐ
# 更 漏 子

## Wēn Tíng-yùn
## 温 庭 筠

Yù lú xiāng, hóng là lèi
玉 爐 香　　紅 蠟 淚，
piān zhào huà táng qiū sǐ
偏 照 畫 堂 秋 思。

Méi cuì buó, bìn yún cān
眉 翠 薄 鬢 雲 殘，
yè cháng qīn zhěn hán
夜 長 衾 枕 寒。

Wú tóng shù, sān gēng yǔ
梧 桐 樹 三 更 雨，
bù dào lí qíng gèng kǔ
不 道 離 情 更 苦。
Yī yè yè, yī shēng shēng
一 葉 葉，一 聲 聲，
kōng jiē dī dào míng
空 階 滴 到 明。

# Song of Hourglass at Night

by Wen Ting-yun


The joss stick smokes in an incense burner,
Red Wax candle glistens with tears,
Lighting up partially,
My autumn thought in the painted hall.
Green colour on eyebrows are small,
Cloud-like hair on temples are chaotic.
Night is so long that,
Quilt and pillows are cold.

On a Chinese parasol tree rain falls,
In the dead of night, regardless of,
The parting feelings harder.
A leaf after a leaf,
One sound and another,
Dripping till dawn,
Pitter-pattering on the empty stairs.

# Appreciation

This is a ci-poem writing of a lady's worry when she is alone in her boudoir in autumn and isn't able to sleep at night. The first part writes the substances in the room and the sting from them which influenced the woman's mood. The first two sentences describes the night scene of the room. " The joss stick smokes, wax candle glistens ". It looks as if it would make one feel happy. But the word " tears " sowed the seeds of grief. The third sentence suddenly introduces a worrisome circumstance, The scenery above, all at once, became the heroine's distress. Originally she had someone to think of who was not present and was unable to enjoy this autumn evening with her. Everything in the room was but an empty shell, just making her feel desolate. " Lighting up partially " were the intense feeling eruptted simultaneously. The expression was very strong. It seemed to her that everything in the room was unbearable. Such unreasonable thought was the result of deep love. The following three sentences: " Green colour on eyebrows are small. Cloud-like hair on temples are chaotic. The night is so long that quilt and pillows are cold. " write of the lady in the room being unable to sleep. When she tossed and turned in bed, the green colour on her eyebrows was wiped off so it became small. Her cloud-like hair was in disorder. Because she was sleepless, she felt that the quilt and pillows were cold.

The second part describes the sound of rain outside the room. In autumn the leaves of the Chinese parasol tree wither. The rain falls on them, which sound is especially loud and clear, more so in the dead of night. " Regardless of " means that the rain did not have any sympathy with this woman's feelings. It seemed deliberately to make things difficult for her, so, she was in an extremly awkward situation.

The last three sentences are the climax of the poem which describes the heroine listening to the sound of rain who felt very much embarrassed. The dripping was till dawn. Naturally the listener did not

fall asleep all night. The empty stairs added the feeling of the sound.
What would her mood be? Reading these three sentences, one
seems to hear the dripping of the rain which were beating on her
heart.

# Nǔ Guān Zǐ
# 女 冠 子

Wèi Zhuāng
韋　莊

Zuó yè yè bàn
昨　夜　夜　半，

Zhěn shàng fēn míng mèng jiàn
枕　上　分　明　夢　見。

Yǔ duō shī
語　多　時，

yī jiù táo huā miàn
依　舊　桃　花　面，

pín dī lǐu yè méi
頻　低　柳　葉　眉。

Bàn xīu hái bàn xǐ
半　羞　還　半　喜，

yù qù yòu yī yī
欲　去　又　依　依。

Jué lái zhī shì mèng
覺　來　知　是　夢，

bú shèng bēi
不　勝　悲。

# Song of a Woman's Crown

by Wei Zhuang

Last night, the mid of it,
On pillows I clearly dreamt of you.
For a long time you chatted.
Still your face was like a peach blossom,
Often you lowered your eyebrows,
As leaves of willow.

Half shy and half delighted,
You desired to leave but,
Were reluctant to part.
I realized it was a dream when I woke up.
I couldn't bear my weep.

# Appreciation

Before " Woman Crown " was adopted as the name of a tune of ci-poem, it had been the name of a tune of Qu in Tang Dynasty. " Woman Crown " means woman taoist priest. This tune originally sang the praises of woman taoist priests' manner. The woman taoist priests at that time were prostitutes rather than religion believers. So this tune always describes women taoist priests postures and looks, or wind, flowers, snow and moon. This ci-poem describes the mood of a man's yearning to see his lover. He was separated from her. He had only the dream following her. So this ci-poem started from his dream and ended by the awakening. In the middle it writes of the sight he saw in the dream.

The first two sentences: " Last night, the mid of it, on pillows I clearly dreamt of you. " tells us that he yearned to see her every day, so he dreamt of her at night. The following sentences: " For a long time you chatted. Still your face was like a peach blossom, Often you lowered your eyebrows as leaves of willow. " describes her manner which were the same as before. From his deep impression we learn he loved her very much.

The second part of the ci-poem continues to describe her manner. The difference between these two parts was the poet here described the change of her inner feelings. " Half shy and half delighted " referred to her happy state of mind and excitement, " desired to leave but were reluctant to part " referred to her loathing to part from him, and her ample tenderness. He seemed to be writing the other side, but was really writing himself, writing his own experience. Soon came the time to part. Because he loved her deeply, he was afraid of their separation. So when he dreamt of " you desired to leave but were reluctant to part " . he awoke suddenly from dream at this very moment. Till the reality sobered him up, he realised it was only a dream. He not only felt lonely, but knew that she was not here. " He couldn't bear his weep "

This ci-poem was very plain. It described every thing frankly. This was the characteristic of Wei Zhang's style, so was his strong point in ci-poetry.

## A Brief Account of the Author's Life

Wei Zhang (836 – 910) styled himself Duan Ji. He was a native of Chang An, Du Ling (now the south east of Xi An). He lived in the Tang Dynasty when it was proceeding from weakness into destruction. Then came the Five Dynasties, the ten countries splitting apart and the setting up of a separatist regime by armed force. He was a successful candidate in the highest imperial examinations when he was 59. He helped Wang Jian constructed a small court of " Former Shu ". Because he wrote a long narrative poem of " Song of a Qin Lady ", which reflected the Yellow Nest Uprising at Chang An, and exerted a tremendous influence, so he was called a scholar of " Song of a Qin Lady ". He enjoyed equal popularity with Wen Ting-yun in the world of ci-poetry, and both were called " Wen Wei ". He was the representative writer of " the School between Flowers " of ci-poets. He compiled " A Collection of Huan Hua ".

# Yè Jīn Mén
# 謁 金 門

Wèi Zhuāng
韋　莊

Chūn yǔ zú
春　雨　足，

rǎn jiù yī xī xīn lù
染　就　一　溪　新　綠。

Liǔ wài fēi lái shuāng yǔ yù
柳　外　飛　來　雙　羽　玉，

nòng qíng xiāng duì yù
弄　晴　相　對　浴。

Lóu wài cuì lián gāo zhóu
樓　外　翠　簾　高　軸，

yǐ biàn lán gān jǐ qǔ
倚　遍　闌　干　幾　曲。

Yún dàn shuǐ píng yān shù cù
雲　淡　水　平　煙　樹　簇，

cùn xīn qiān lǐ mù
寸　心　千　里　目。

38

# Call on the Golden Gate

by Wei Zhuang


Spring rain is plentiful.
It dyes the stream small,
With new green full.
Outside the willows,
Come white gulls,
Like jades in pairs,
Under the sunshine,
They are sporting,
Face to face bathing.

Upstairs
Green curtains,
Are rolled up high.
How many zigzag parapets,
Have been leaning by?
Clouds are pale.
Water surface is smooth.
Smoky trees clustered.
Gazing into the distance,
My feelings are far-seeing eyes.

# Apperciation

This is an extremely perfect ci-poem. The first part of it describes the scenery. After a new rain, the small stream was full of green water. The white gulls in pairs were sporting under the sunshine. The scenery was really like a painting. It was flourishing too. Because the ci-poet used those verbs: " dyes, come, are sporting ", the general appearance of the picture is permeated with vitality. The second part of this ci-poem expresses a woman's emotion. She rolled up green curtains and leaned on the parapets. Her husband must not have been at home for a long time. When the green curtains were rolled up high, her field of vision would be widened, she could see further. The second sentence " How many zigzag parapets have been leaning by? " described that she had leaned on the parapets for a long time and so her mood was uncertain. These two sentences all stress the parting emotion. The last two sentences: " Clouds are pale, Water surface is smooth. Smoky trees clustered. Gazing into the distance. My feelings are far-seeing eyes. " describes the sight in the woman's eyes, which is boundless, distant and hazy. Though they describe the scenery, they really describe the woman's miserable situation. Using words " feelings " and " far-seeing eyes " the ci-poet expresses how deep and intense the parting emotion was, which is easier to be seen.

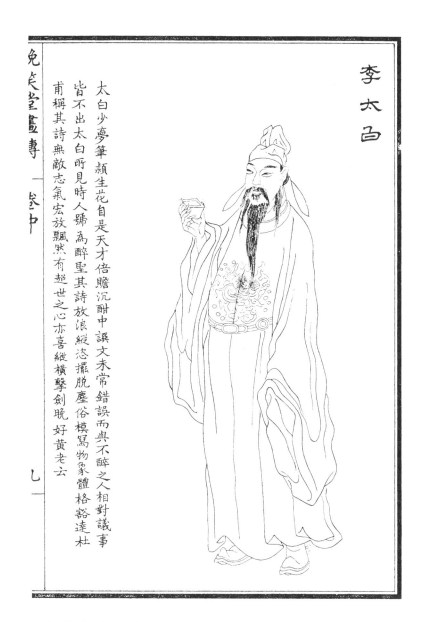

李太白

太白少夢筆頭生花自是天才倍贍沉酣中謨文未嘗錯誤而與不醉之人相對議事
皆不出太白所見時人蹄為醉聖其詩放浪縱恣擺脫塵俗模寫物象體格豁達杜
甫稱其詩無敵志氣宏放飄然有超世之心亦喜縱橫擊劍晚好黃老云

兒民堂畫傳 卷中 乙

Li Bai：One of the greatest ci-poets of Tang Dynasty

# Shēng Chá Zǐ
# 生　查　子

Níu Xī-jì
牛希濟

Chūn shān yān yù shōu
春　山　煙　欲　收，

tiān dàn xīng xī xiǎo
天　淡　星　稀　小。

Cán yuè liǎn biān míng
殘　月　臉　邊　明，

bié lèi lín qīng xiǎo
別　淚　臨　清　曉。

Yǔ yǐ duō, qíng wèi liǎo
語　已　多，情　未　了。

Huí shǒu yóu chóng dào
回　首　猶　重　道：

Jì dé lǜ luó qún
記　得　綠　羅　裙，

chù chù lián fāng cǎo
處　處　憐　芳　草。

# Song of Fresh Berries

by Niu Xi-ji

The mist over spring mountains will disappear.
The sky is pale, stars are fewer and minor.
By the face is the falling moon bright,
At early dawn are parting tears present.

Words have been given a lot,
But loves will not be settled.
Turning head, she still said:
" Remember the green silk skirt,
From place to place,
Have tender affection for fragrant grasses. "

# Appreciation

This is a ci-poem expressing parting feelings. The first two sentences tell us the circumstances in which the characters move about. The mist covering the spring mountain would retreat. The sky became pale and stars were fewer. These were the scenery of early morning. The falling moon had not set yet. The pale moonlight passed through the window as if it were by her face illuminating her warm tears rolling down. The ci-poem does not describe the character from the frontage, but take advantage of the moonlight which seems full of tenderness but merciless, to discover and to portray the character, which is detailed. Such description is not only clever but leaves space for imagination. This pair of lovers might have wept face to face in the early morning. Hence under the author's pen, the moon seemed to have human feelings, it brightened by her face. How fine and smooth was the description! We have to grasp with admiration at his skill.

When two lovers are parting, they often have a lot to say. They will recall the happy past, pour out their heart or make a solemn pledge of love. So the first sentence of the second part said: " Words have been given a lot, But loves will not be settled. " The author utilized " Remember the green silk skirt, From place to place, Have tender affection for fragrant grasses. " for concluding remarks, which was a highly artistic condensation. Because of the woman beloved, he loved all the things related to her and led to think of her. Such psychological state can only be produced when one loves deeply. Niu Xi-ji learnt it from his personal experience and caught this special psychological state to express such sincere love, which may be said having great originality. There were fragrant grasses everywhere. Thinking of green silk skirt, he would have tender affection for the grasses. On the contrary, seeing fragrant grasses, he would think of the green silk skirt, too. These are two sides of a thing, which express a man travelling in a place far away from home having a love unforgetable to his beloved. As a result of these concluding sentences, this ci-poem is highly appraised.

# A Brief Account of the Author's Life

Niu Xi-ji is a native of West Long (now the south east of Gansu Province). When he was born and died was not known. In Former Shu and Later Tang he was government officials. He was good at poems. In "A Collection of Ci-poem between Flowers" eleven of his ci- poems were collected.

# Nán Xiāng Zǐ
# 南　　鄉　　子

Lǐ Xún
李　珣

Chéng cǎi fǎng, guò lián táng
乘　彩　舫，過　蓮　塘，

zhào gē jīng qǐ shuì yuān yāng
棹　歌　驚　起　睡　鴛　鴦。

Yóu nǚ dài xiāng wēi bàn xiào
遊　女　帶　香　偎　伴　笑，

zhēng yāo tiǎo
爭　窈　窕，

jìng zhé tuán hé zhē wǎn zhào
竟　折　團　荷　遮　晚　照。

# Song of the Southern Native Place

by Li Xun


In a gaily-painted pleasure-boat,
A group of girl tourists,
Are riding through the lotus pond,
Oar songs startled,
The sleeping mandarin ducks.
Young girls with fragrant girdles, *
Laughing, lean upon one another,
Striving to be slender,
They compete with each other,
Breaking round lotuses,
The late sunlight to cover.

---

*For line 6, and 7 of this ci-poem, " Young girls with fragrant girdles, laughing, lean upon one another, " another copy writes as " With fragrant girdles the tourist girls laughing, lean upon other person. " Mr Yu Zhong Zhan wrote a note for this line.

          ⊙ ⊙⊙   ⊙●

It says: " 帶香遊女偎人笑 ". So we see that the level or oblique tones of this line in this tune are rather free.

# Appreciation

This is a ci-poem writing of young girls go boating on a lotus pond in summer. Either scenery or customs, the poet all wrote vividly. At the very beginning he said: " A group of girl tourists are riding through the lotus pond in a gaily-painted pleasure boat. " This sentence spread a bright and clean picture to readers. The gaily-painted pleasure boat had various colours, especially red, which went through the boundless green lotus pond. Red and green, set each other off, showing a very beautiful scene. The next sentence: " Oar songs startled the sleeping mandarin ducks " matched a sound for this moving picture. Up to now the ci-poem keep straight on writing the scenery, it does not describe the person on boat. Only from " The young girls with fragrant girdles lean upon one another, laughing ", the heroines appeares. Because oar songs startled the sleeping mandarin ducks under the lotus, the girl tourists laughed. What did they laughed at? How did they laugh? They leant upon one another. These words describe the young girls' attitude of laughing. These were naughty, sweet and simple, slightly bashful laughs. Whether they laughed at the mandarin ducks' simple minded manner or by seeing theirs flying in pairs they aroused a sweet dream of love so beamed with a laugh or for some other reasons else, we did not know and needed not to know. In a word, these were laughs having ease of mind, innocent laughs, laughs interlocking sweet and hope, laughs of women not having been bound up by the yoke of the feudal ethical code. Such free laughs were few in ancient China, so they were extremly touching. The last two sentences express the young girls' liveliness and loveliness. Though it was in summer, towards evening, the sun would not be hot, the girls competed with each other for breaking the round lotuses to cover the late sun-light. In these actions of playing, young girls' gracefulness was manifesting themselves fully. Here " striving " and " compete " two words were used perfectly. They express that the young girls broke the lotuses not to cover the sunshine but to express their youthful beauty and vigour. Just think, a group of young girls in colourful dresses on a gaily painted pleasure boat, proping green round lotuses up. Weren't the postures very lovely? The poet caught this sight intelligently in two and three strokes, the young girls' beautiful picture was soon reflected on an evening background. This is a very succinct sketch, which displays the author's excellent artistic expression.

## A Brief Account of Author's Life

Li Xun (about 855 – about 930) styled himself De Run. He lived in Zi Zhou(now Sichuan Province San Tai county). His younger sister was a wife of King of Su. He was a noted poet and was especially good at ci-poem. He was an important ci-poet of " School between Flowers ". He compiled " A Collection of Qiong Yao ", now no longer extant, but his ci-poems were seen in selected works of " Hua Jian " and " Zun Qian ". " Poems All Round Tang Dynasty " collected 54 pieces of his ci-poems. His style of ci-poem was clear, bright and beautiful but not ornate.

# Dìng Fēng Bō
# 定　風　波

Lǐ Xún
李　珣


Zhì zài yān xiá mù yǐn lún
志 在 煙 霞 慕 隱 淪，
gōng chéng guī kàn wǔ hú chūn
功　成　歸　看　五　湖　春。
Yī yè zhōu zhōng yín fú zuì
一 葉 舟 中 吟 復 醉，
yún shuǐ
雲　水。
Cǐ shí fāng shí zì yóu shēn
此 時 方 識 自 由 身。


Huā dǎo wéi lín ōu zuò lǚ
花　島　爲　鄰　鷗　作　侶，
shēn chù
深　處。
Jīng nián bù jiàn shì cháo rén
經 年 不 見 市 朝 人，
yǐ dé xī yí wéi (miào) zhǐ
已 得 希 夷*微（妙）* 旨，
qián xǐ
潛　喜。
Hé yī huì dài jué xiān chén
荷 衣 蕙 帶 絕 纖 塵。

50

# Calming the Disturbance

by Li Xun


Having a will of mist and cloud,
Fan Li loved seclusion.
He returned
To admire Wu Hu Spring,
though succeeded.
On a leaf boat,
He drank and recited,
Between water and cloud.
At this moment he just realized.
The value of freedom.

Flower island was neighbor,
In the depths, gull was partner.
All the year round he did not meet person in
power.
He has obtained Xi Yi delicate realm and,
Inwardly rejoiced for them.
He dressed lotus garment and orchid ribbon,
Did not get a speck on them.

---

* Chen Tuan, styled himself Xi Yi, lived in Song Dynasty, who knew abstruse philosophy. Xi Yi delicate realm refers to his philosophic realm.
On the basis of 《 A Collection of Zun Qian(尊前)》, after the word wei 微,
there is a word miao(妙), which was missing in this ci-poem, so supplied.
* * The two parts of this tune rhymed level tone are confined to one rhyme
to the end, rhymed oblique tone should rhyme three rhymes respectively, according to the ci-poem rules of Wan Shu(萬樹《 詞律 》, which is different
from this one.

# Appreciation

The writer of this ci-poem indicates his own will by making use of Fan Li's experience. Fan Li helped King of Yue (Gou Jian) eliminated the kingdom of Wu. After his success, he secluded himself from society and went boating on the Five Lakes to admire the beauty of nature. Li Xun thought him noble and expressed admiration of him. So at the beginning of this poem, he wrote straightly that Fan Li had a will of mist and cloud, and loved seclusion to extel his noble qualities. " Mist and cloud " meant the smoke and rosy clouds between mountain and water. " Seclusion " meant to conceal one's identity. Li Xun highly praised Fan Li, in reality, expressed his own wish. The second sentence said: " Though he succeeded he returned to admire Wu Hu Spring ". Then he continued writing the pleasure of the life of retirement. " On a leaf boat ", he wandered about unhurriedly in the lake, " drank and recited poetry ", amidst water and cloud, he enjoyed the scenery as much as he liked. How happy he was! The conclusion of the first part: " Only at this moment he realized the value of freedom " reflected the recluses' free and unrestrained life and the author's weariness outlook on life.

The second part continue stating the happiness of living in seclusion. " Flower island was neighbour, gull was partner. " " In the depth " means live in the depth of strange mountains and water. The recluse was peaceful and comfortable. There he did not meet persons being after fame and position all the year round. He could reach such a state because " he has obtained Xi Yi delicate realm ", (that is Chen Tuan's philosophy). Thus he felt joyful. The last sentence, he dresses " lotus garment and orchit ribbon ". Such costume is the adornment of god. This description is just a figure of speech, which is used to describe the recluse's noble and unsullied. The author admired seclusion and had the same will of mist and cloud as Fan Li. Fan Li lived in seclusion after he succeeded. He found Gou Jian a person could go through thick and thin together but could not share peace and happiness. So he firmly went into retirement. He did this starting from initiative. Li Xun did not do a deed of merit but suffered the pain of national subjugation. Though they all went into retirement, their mood were different.

# Yú Měi Rén
## 虞 美 人

Lǐ Yù
李 煜

Chūn huā qiū yuè hé shí liǎo
春 花 秋 月 何 時 了，
wǎng shì zhī duō shǎo
往 事 知 多 少。
Xiǎo lóu zuó yè yòu dōng fēng
小 樓 昨 夜 又 東 風，
gù guó bù kān huí shǒu yuè míng zhōng
故 國 不 堪 回 首 月 明 中。

Diāo lán yù qì yīng yóu zài
雕 欄 玉 砌 應 猶 在，
zhǐ shì zhū yán gǎi
只 是 朱 顏 改。
Wèn jūn néng yǒu jǐ duō chóu
問 君 能 有 幾 多 愁，
qià shì yī jiāng chūn shuǐ xiàng dōng líu
恰 似 一 江 春 水 向 東 流。

# The Beautiful Lady Yu

by Li Yu


When will spring flowers and autumn moon
be buried?
How many past events well up in my memory?
Last night an eastern wind blew again on my
dormitory,
In the bright moonlight,
I could not bear to look back my former country.

The carved balustrades and marble steps
should still be there,
But the vermilion faces must be pale.
If asked, how much distress is in the heart?
Just like a full river of spring water flowing east.

# Appreciation

This ci-poem was written after Li Yu had been captured in Bian Jing. It began with " When will spring flowers and autumn moon be buried? " Why he wanted the happy days to end? Because: whenever he saw the spring flowers and autumn moon, memories of the past would well up in his mind, he would think of the happy days in South Tang and would find it unbearable to recall. When east wind was swaying and the moon was bright, his heart was bleeding. Yet he couldn't help looking back. " The carved balustrades and marble steps should still be there. " means the building of his palace should remain as before. Because of distress, the looks of his people must be thin and pallid. How miserable it was! So the poet continued to write: " If asked, how much distress is in the heart? Just like a full river of spring water flowing east. " " A full river " referred to the Yangtze River. The distress was likened to the Yangtze River flowing endlessly. Jin Ling was beside the Yangtze. The poet wrote Yangtze because he cherished the memory of the old country deeply. Li Yu's birthday was the seventh evening in July. On that day he asked some former singers to play a stringed musical instrument in his dormitory. The sound was heard outside. Tai Zong of the Song Dynasty knew it, he flew into a rage. Someone reported that Li Yu wrote " Last night an eastern wind blew again on my dormitory " and " how much distress is in the heart? " " Just like a full river of spring water flowing east. " etc. Tai Zong thought that Li Yu wanted to rebel, so he killed him with poison. This ci-poem was written by blood. Li Yu wrote such a ci-poem not only to express his own distress, but to have a highly artistic condensation. It summarized the pain of the people in a conquered nation. This was the outstanding point of this ci-poem. It had a great influence on the later generations.

# A Brief Account of the Author's Life

Li Yu (937 – 978), styled himself Chong Guang. At first he was named Cong Jia. Zhong Yin was his assumed name. He was the sixth son of Zhong Zhu in South Tang. He succeeded to the throne in 961 and was called Hou Zhu in History. He was a native of Xu Zhou. He reigned over his kingdom for fifteen years. After he had ascended the throne, he revered Song Dynasty, sought pleasure and momentary ease. So the troops of Song Dynasty broke through Jing Ling (now Nanjing). He surrendered and was captured in Bian Jing (Now Kai Feng). It is said on his birthday, the seventh evening in July, Li Yu asked some of his former singers to play an instrument in his domitory and wrote the ci poem: "Last night an eastern wind blew again on my dormitory." "Just like a full river of spring water flowing east." Song Tai Zong, killed him with poison. When Li Yu was a king, he wrote poems reflecting his life in ease and comfort, having a weak and dissipated style. After he surrendered his poems reflected the pain of the people in a conquered nation. While the range of subject enlarged, the artistic conception was magnificently conceived. The emotion of his ci-poems was sincere and rich in artistic appeal. He achieved great success for the Five Dynasties' ci-poems of the last years of the Tang Dynasty.

# Qīng Píng Lè
# 清　平　樂

Lǐ Yù
李煜

Bié lái chūn bàn
別來春半，

chù mù róu cháng duàn
觸目柔腸斷。

Qì xià luò méi rú xuě luàn
砌下落梅如雪亂，

fú liǎo yī shēn huán mǎn
拂了一身還滿。

Yàn lái yīn xìn wú píng
雁來音信無憑，

lù yáo guī mèng nán chéng
路遙歸夢難成。

Lí hèn qià rú chūn cǎo
離恨恰如春草，*

gèng xíng géng yuǎn huán shēng
更行更遠還生。

# Pure Serene Music

by Li Yu

Since we parted,
Spring has half lost.
Every where I look,
My tender heart breaks,
Fallen plum blossoms,
Like snow flakes,
Whirl around below steps,
No sooner brushed away,
Than covering me over again.

The wild geese come,
But with me you weren't in correspondence
The road is so long,
That your homesick dream can't be done.
Separation sorrow is like grasses in spring,
However distantly I wander,
I find it growing no end.

---

\* In sentence " 離恨恰如春草 ", the first, third and fifth words may be level or oblique tones, the second, fourth and sixth words are oblique, level and oblique tones according to the rules but some great poets may not follow the rules.

# Appreciation

This ci-poem wrote with parting emotion. In 966, Li Yu's younger brother, Cong Shan entered the state of Song, but was not allowed to return. Li Yu missed him very much, writing this ci-poem. At the beginning of this ci poem, the poet pointed out the particularity of the matter and the season. The middle of spring was a time of sunlit and enchanting. Why did he say: " My tender heart breaks "? Because his brother was in the enemy's hand, his fate hanged in the balance, so everywhere the poet looked, there was a shadow on it. Why did he write about the scenery? " Fallen plum blossoms like snow flakes whirl around below steps, No sooner brushed away than covering me over again. " These two sentences described a cool and silent tableau. The plum blossoms were falling from the sky, a man with an emaciated look stood in the snow white world. What did it mean? The picture reflected the poet's lonely heart. In such a fine season such beautiful flowers were merely falling. What a pity! Looking at the falling flowers, he must have felt the grief of life. So these two sentences either expressed the fact, or his own idea. The scenery served the feelings, feelings were superior to scenery.

The second part writes of the parting. The first sentence said: " The wild geese come, But with me you weren't in correspondence. " Judged by scenery, this was a change, judged by feelings, this went a step further. The ancients said, the wild geese could bring letters, but now they had come, no letter followed. The fact while the wild geese came, neither the dear one nor a letter appeared, could only add sorrow to the poet's heart. Then his pen turned to write the dear one. He was far far away from home, lonely and in danger. Even his home sick dream wasn't able to enrich the native land. How couldn't the poet help thinking of him? The missing would be endless. So he wrote: " Separation sorrow is like grasses in spring, however distantly I wander, I find it growing no end. " His sorrow was

60

likened to the grasses at the end of the world, continuously, boundlessly. How lively, vivid, natural and suitable it was.

# Xiāng Jiàn Huān
# 相　見　歡

Lǐ Yù
李煜

Lín huā xiè liǎo chūn hóng
林　花　謝　了　春　紅，

tài cōng cōng
太　匆　匆，

wú nài zhāo lái hán yǔ
無　奈　朝　來　寒　雨，

wǎn lái fēng
晚　來　風。

Yān zhī lèi
胭　脂　淚，

xiāng líu zuì
相　留　醉，

jǐ shí chōng
幾　時　重。

Zì shì rén shēng cháng hèn
自　是　人　生　長　恨，

shuǐ cháng dōng
水　長　東！

# Joy of Meeting

by Li Yu


The forest blossoms have withered,
Losing their spring crimson.
Why all this hurry?
Having no choice
They stood the cold rain at dawn,
And the winds night borne.

Rouge-stained tears,
Ask to stay each other,
To be intoxicated together.
When will they reappear?
These are life's endless regrets,
As the endless river
Flows east forever.

# Appreciation

This ci-poem was an extempore lyric. The poet described the natural scene, the last days of spring and the withered flowers to express his disappointed and disconsolate mind.

In the first part, the poet described that under the destruction of the cold rain and strong wind, the forest blossoms faded and fell rapidly. Spring left in a hurry. Through this description he expressed between the lines his extreme sorrow: life was short and difficult, good times did not last long.

The first sentence " The forest blossoms have withered, losing their spring crimson " drew a picture of the remnant of spring. Looking at such a sight who wouldn't feel sorry? The emotion resided in the scenery. The feelings were strong. " Why all this hurry? " These several words made the morale of sorrow even more stronger. The last sentence of the first part said:
" Having no choice they stood the cold rain at dawn and the winds night borne " , which gave the reason. Nature changes regularly but is also changeable. Sometimes it is fine, sometimes it rains, sometimes warm, sometimes cold and capricious. They destroy the flowers. Here morning and evening meant every morning and every evening. The frequency was high. They gave forest blossoms cruel and merciless blows. The flowers were unable to resist. The poet's experience was just like theirs. So he was not only pitied the flowers but was also pityful. The first part both gave the reason why the flowers withered and expressed the poet's lament. Though he wrote these thoughts, he really told of his own experience.

The second part expressed that good times would not come again and the hate for suffering in life. The first sentence:
" Rouge – stained tears " was the application of personification skill. Rouge is the pink powder decorated on women's faces. Here it referred to the withered forest blossoms. Carmine tear

drops referred to the red flowers drifting from place to place, wetted by the cold rain that was blown by the evening wind, just as the beauty's tears which went down with the carmine when she felt extremely sorrow. The forest blossom, losing their spring crimson, could not have shed tears. Tears have been entrusted to them by the poet. From this point of view, these tears were not only the sadness of the forest blossoms but also the tears of the poet. He recalled his past emperor life, which was ruined too early under the sword and spear when threatened by the soldiers of Song Dynasty, he shed sorrowful tears.

" Ask each other to stay and to be intoxicated together. " Who asked whom to stay? Did the flowers ask themselves, ask the poet or did the poet ask flowers? Savour the meaning of this ci-poem, we may say, all did. Flowers wished that they could stay longer though the rain was cold and the wind was strong. They were unwilling to wither early. Flowers also wanted the poet to stay. The forest blossoms were sheding tears as if asking the poet to see them once more, not to cruel-heartedly leave them alone. As for the poet's asking flowers to stay, he really did so. He lingered with the flowers not willing to leave. He wished that the flowers could always blossom and live long. He wanted the flowers and the spring to stay. It also meant he hoped his life as emperor could be long. What did " to be intoxicated " mean? The forest blossoms lost their spring crimson. But when they were flourishing, they had been intoxicated with self-satisfaction. Now, though withered, they still reveled in their former beauty. So did the poet. When he was a king, he enjoyed many flowers, intoxicated with his former life. Merely the good scenery had difficulty reappearing. The past life had gone, never to return. So he asked: " When will they reappear? " Outwardly, the poet asked when the flowers would reappear but inwardly he really asked when his emperor life would return again? These were difficult to realize. So he said: " These are life's endless regrets, as the endless river flowing east forever. " The two " endless " expressed his extremely deep sorrow.

# Dāo Liàn Zǐ Lìng
# 捣 練 子 令

Lǐ Yù
李 煜

Shēn yuàn jìng, xiǎo tíng kōng
深 院 靜, 小 庭 空,

duàn xù hán zhēn duàn xù fēng
斷 續 寒 砧 斷 續 風。

Wú nài yè cháng rén bú mèi
無 奈 夜 長 人 不 寐,

shù shēng hé yuè dào lián lóng
數 聲 和 月 到 簾 櫳。

# Song of Pounding Silk Floss

by Li Yu

The deep court is silent,
Empty is the little yard.
Off and on go the taps
On hammering block cold,
Off and on goes the wind.
Having no choice is
The man's wakefulness with the length of night,
A few sounds together with the moonlight,
Come to the curtain and window of mine.

# Appreciation

This was a ci-poem with the original meaning. " Bai Lian " was an ancient silk woven fabric. In process of production, it would undergo thumps with a club on a hammering block. This work was done by women generally. The tune of this ci-poem got the name from the content of pounding silk floss.

The poet wrote of his own impatience and worry through the description of an insomniac hearing of the thumping sound at night. He arranged a very quiet and lonesome, hollow and in-different circumstance for his intranquil mood. The first two sentences seemed duplicates at first glance, but really not. The first one appealed to the sense of hearing, while the second one, the sense of sight. Though the ears were listening and the eyes looking, nothing was heard and seen. Thus the words silent and empty not only gave the difference in feeling, but showed us the poet's painstaking use of words. " Deep court " expressed the inhabitant departing far from the hubbub. " Little yard " described the place where the poet lived was not " carved beams and painted rafters " , but an empty small yard, poor, quiet and hollow. These two sentences seemed to write scenery, actually to set off the hero's heart as lonely and bored. Only in such a quiet small court could the thumping sound carried here by the continual wind be heard by the poet. The third sentence was the core of this ci-poem. Since in an-cient times the thumping sounds on a hummering block had been the material of yearning between lovers and a recall of the past, this ci poem was without exception. It was written from the angle of the man hearing the pounding sounds. The poet used two off-and-on's, but their meanings were different. Gen-erally speaking, thumping on a hammering block always has rhythm. Between the two thumps there was a short intermit-tence. Because the wind was sometimes strong and sometimes weak, sometimes existed and sometimes not, only some sounds were sent to the small court. It was because the wind was continual, the thumping sound occurred now and then which was sometimes audible, sometimes inaudible. The poet wrote this which made the depressed static state appealing to the sense of hearing live.

The last two sentences read: " Having no choice is the man's wakefulness with the length of night. A few sounds together with the moonlight come to the window and curtain of mine. " These sentences linked the sense of hearing and the sense of sight together, voice and countenance mingled — — the clear light of the autumn moon and the thumping sound merged into one, which stirred up the poet's feeling. He did not make a vivid description, enormously exaggerated, but used monotonous thumping sound and simple moonlight to win the reader's sympathy with his loneliness and sleeplessness. This was the skill of Li Yu's ci-poem. His simple straight forward style of writing was praised all over the world.

# Yú Měi Rén
# 虞　美　人

Lǐ Yù
李　煜

Fēng húi xiǎo yuàn tíng wú lù
風　回　小　院　庭　蕪　綠，

lǐu yǎn chūn xiāng xù
柳　眼　春　相　續。

Píng lán bàn rì dú wú yán
憑　欄　半　日　獨　無　言，

yī jìu zhú shēng xīn yùe sì dāng nián
依　舊　竹　聲　新　月　似　當　年。

Shēng gē wèi sàn zūn léi zài
笙　歌　未　散　尊　罍　在，

chí miàn bīng chū jiě
池　面　冰　初　解。

Zhú míng xiāng àn huà táng shēn
燭　明　香　暗　畫　堂　深，

mǎn bìn qīng shuāng cán xuě sī nán rén
滿　鬢　清　霜　殘　雪　思　難　任。

70

# The Beautiful Lady Yu

by Li Yu

Wind has returned to the small yard,
Weeds became green,
Willow leaves like sleeping eyes,
Continued the spring.
For a long time without a word,
I was alone on rails leaning.
As they were in those years,
Bamboo sound and the new moon remained
unchanging.

Playing and singing were not over,
Urn-shaped wine-vessels still there,
Ice on the surface of the pool began to disappear.
The candles are bright, joss sticks dim,
The painted hall seems deeper.
My hair are all white on temple,
Like cold frost and survival snow,
The weight of my grief is hard to hold.

# Appreciation

This ci-poem was written when Li Yu was captured and was detained at Bianjing (another name for Kaifeng in Henan Province), which reflected his life in detention. The ci-poem began with "Wind has returned to the small yard, Weeds became green, Willow leaves like sleeping eyes continued the spring." Such willow leaves grow in succession when spring comes. This description revealed spring information of the small yard. The writing was very fine which was the poet's observation. From this description we can see that he was very lonely. Recalling the happy life before surrender, he leaned on the rails without a word, which disclosed his suffering in thinking of his old country. He still wanted to mediate for himself, so he said: "Bamboo sound and the New moon remained unchanging, as they were in those years." But contrast his present situation with his happiness in his old country were they the same? What would he think?

The next part was about his life in the house that had been granted to him. He was still able to have prostitutes "playing and singing" for him. He also had wine to drink. Spring came. The ice on the surface of the pool began to disappear. Could we say his hard life was like the ice, which would disappear? The poet said: "The candles are bright, joss sticks dim, the painted hall seems deeper. My hair on the temples is all white, Like cold frost and survival snow, The weight of my grief is hard to hold." The poet used "The candles are bright, joss sticks dim." to set off "The painted hall seems deeper", and "My hair on the temples is all white, like cold frost and survival snow." to set off "Ice on the surface of the pool began to disappear". "The painted hall seems deeper" was words with a deepened tone. It seemed "the playing and singing" did not make him happy, just consoled himself in his lonely time, so he felt that the painted hall seemed deeper. That the ice melted meant the spring had come, but to him

72

the spring had gone forever. He showed this for, he was only forty, but his hair was all white, like cold frost and survival snow. One can well perceive how deep his pain in national subjugation was. So he wrote " the weight of my grief is hard to hold. " We see perfectly well what he meant.

# Wū Yè Tí
# 烏 夜 啼*

Lǐ Yù
李 煜

Wú yán dú shàng xī lóu
無 言 獨 上 西 樓，

yuè rú gōu
月 如 鈎。

Jí mò wú tóng shēn yuàn
寂 寞 梧 桐 深 院，

suǒ qīng qiū
鎖 清 秋。

Jiǎn bù duàn, lǐ huán luàn
剪 不 斷 理 還 亂，

shì lí chōu
是 離 愁。

Bié shì yī bān zī wèi, zài xīn tóu
別 是 一 般 滋 味 在 心 頭。

# Crows Crying at Night

by Li Yu

Wordlessly,
I climbed the Western Tower alone.
Like a hook is the moon.
Lonely Chinese parasols
And the deep courtyard,
Lock the cool autumn.

Scissors can't be severed,
Sorted out, again it tangles,
That's the sorrow of separation,
With a flavour all its own for the heart.

---

* The name of this tune is also called " Joy of Meeting " .

# Appreciation

This ci-poem was regarded as a work of Li Yu after his surrender. Li Yu was a dissolute king. After he was captured, he lived a prisoner's life. He suffered humiliation and shed tears day and night. This ci-poem expressed his thinking about his native land and his hate of being conquered. The tone of writing was very heavy. After a sentence stop he used a very sad rhyme.

The first sentence said: " Wordlessly I climbed the Western Tower alone. " " Wordlessly " made a sketch of Li Yu's sad manner. He had no one to speak with. He was lonely and unhappy. " I climbed the Western Tower alone " explained his action. He walked a step, heaved a sigh. The paces were heavy. On the Western Tower, he saw " The moon like a hook " . This meant it was deep at night. At such a time, Li Yu did not go to bed but climbed the Western Tower alone. Why? His hate was bitter and deep, His state of mind was contradictory and complicated.

" The moon was like a hook. " This sight tallied with the poet's mood. The moon was incomplete. It had a certain emblematic significance. The moonlight was like autumn frost, desolate, cold and lonely. The cold and gloomy moonlight cast its light upon the miserable reality: the poor man, wordlessly climbed the Western Tower alone and also the lost land of his country. Under the cold moonlight, the serious facts of life couldn't be hidden. The poet raised his head, saw the moon like a hook, and bowed his head. He observed the lonely Chinese parasols and the deep courtyard locked the cool autumn. Placing himself in the midst of such an atmosphere, he would surely be heartbroken. In autumn only naked branches remained on the Chinese parasoles. The thin moonlight passing through them sprayed shadows over the ground, cold and in a mess. Though this description expressed the real scene, it was, in fact, the poet's mood too. It contained strong emotional colour. Since the poet was captured, his body and mind were both locked there. In the poet's eyes, the autumn scenery was almost all locked in the deep court, destroyed by his enemy. The word "lock" was not only lively, but also sad, very sad. What was really locked in the court was far more than the autumn. Though "lock" was only a word, it explained the whole state.

The next part spoke bluntly about the poet's distress. The first three sentences said: "Scissor can't be severed, Sorted out, again it tangles. That's the sorrow of separation." "Sorrow" is a subjective abstract thing. The metaphor here made it concrete and easy to feel. The thought which was complicated and couldn't be sorted was likened to a yarn of ramie, inexhaustible and endless. The more you sorted it out, the more it is disordered. The inextricable degree and endless manner was likened to the flowing water which couldn't be severed. This metarphor utilized the visible to contrast the invisible, it made the action of thinking which is invisible and unable to feel get miraculous effects. The concluding sentence:
"With a flavour, all its own for the heart." was the poet's sigh over his unhappy fate. What the poet said was not only the word
"worry" which could be summarized. It seemed a flavour that was difficult to ascertain but could be indistinctively felt. This was using the invisible to contrast the invisible. This invisible was just hard to say or the poet did not want to say. This experience was very deep. The sorrow was very bitter.

# Yè Jīn Mén
# 謁金門

Féng Yán-sì
馮 延巳

Fēng zhà qǐ
風 乍 起，

chuī zhòu yī chí chūn shuǐ
吹 皺 一 池 春 水。

Xián yǐn yuān yāng xiāng jìng lǐ
閒 引 鴛 鴦 香 徑 裏，

shǒu ruó hóng xìng ruǐ
手 挼 紅 杏 蕊。

Dòu yā lán gān biàn yǐ
鬥 鴨 闌 干 遍 倚。

Bì yù sāo tóu xié zhuì
碧 玉 搔 頭 斜 墜。

Zhōng rì wàng jūn jūn bù zhì
終 日 望 君 君 不 至，

jǔ tóu wén què xǐ
舉 頭 聞 鵲 喜。

# Call on the Golden Gate

by Feng Yan-si


A wind suddenly rises,
Which blows crumples
On a pond of spring water.
At leisure,
I lead mandarin ducks,
To fragrant path,
Rubbing the red apricot buds,
In my delicate palms.

Duck fighting balustrades are leaned on all over.
My emerald hairpin is slant and fall.
To the coming of you look forward,
All day long, but you don't
When I raised my head and heard the yell of a magpie,
Happy I felt.

# Appreciaition

This ci-poem wrote the state of an aristocratic lady who was waiting for her lover's coming with anxiety in spring.

At the outset, it said: " A wind suddenly rises, which blows crumples on a pond of spring water. " This sight implied symbolic meaning. Spring breeze rose and fell like waves. The blowing wind rippled the pond water and also broke the heart of the lady. The poet utilized a word " crumple " describing the mood exactly. Since it was a spring wind, not a fierce one, it only rippled the water, did not make roaring waves. The heroine's mood was like the spring water, only in a state of anxiety. In the face of such a bright and beautiful spring, her lover was not there, how could she while away the beautiful scene on this bright day? She had to go for a walk in the fragrant path rubbing the red apricot buds with her hands, and teasing mandarin ducks. Even the mandarin ducks were in pairs. This phenomenon could not but touch the heroine's distressed and love sick heart, cause her envy, and make her feel her fate was inferior to poultry. She picked a red apricot buds carelessly, put it in her palms, broke it slightly into pieces. Through this detail, the ci-poem expressed the heroine's complicated feelings carefully. That was: though she was as beautiful and fragrant as the red apricot bud, her heart was broken into pieces by another pair of hands. How meticulous the description was! How deep were the feelings! It simply described the figure's subconscious field.

The next part said: as she was in such a distressed mood, all the scenery around her could not arouse her interest. Though she leaned on all the balustrades, she was in low spirit. Here, " all over " described what she had was a very hard time. She was laden with anxiety, crestfallen. Because her head was hung down for a long time, her emerald hairpin was slant and fell. She thought of her lover all day long, but he did not come. Suddenly she heard the yell of a magpie. As the proverb goes: " A magpie calls, happy events come. " Could it be that her lover would come? So she raised her head and felt happy.

The description was very careful, mild, succinct and vivid, which was worth learning.

## A Brief Account of the Author's Life

Fen Yan-si (903-960), styled himself Zheng Zhong. He was a native of Guang Ling (now Yang Zhou county, Jiangsu Province). He followed Li Jing (the middle king of the Southern Tang) since his youth. He worked as a minister in Li's court. He was good at rhetoric, skill and writing poems. Though he was rich, he did not stop writing when old. He not only had most ci poems preserved in the ci-poem world of the Southern Tang, but also was a great master of ci-poem in the Later Tang Dynasty. He created an artistic realm of profound, beautiful, grand, restricted, solemn and just style. His ci-poems had a direct influence in the early ci-poem world of Northern Song. He compiled "A Collection of Yang Chun" but no longer extant. Chen Shi-xiu, a scholar of Song Dynasty, compiled another one. He also named it "A Collection of Yang Chun" which preserved a preservation of one hundred and twenty pieces of contemporary ci-poems. Many of them were his works.

# Zuì Táo Yuán
## 醉　桃　源*

Féng Yún-sì

馮　延巳

Nán yuán chūn bàn tà qīng shí
南　園　春　半　踏　青　時，

fēng hé wén mǎ sī
風　和　聞　馬　嘶。

Qīng méi rú dòu lǐu rú méi
青　梅　如　豆　柳　如　眉，

rì cháng hú díe fēi
日　長　蝴　蝶　飛。

Huā lù zhòng, cǎo yān dī
花　露　重　草　煙　低，

rén jiā lián mù chuí
人　家　簾　幕　垂。

Qīu qiān yōng kùn jiě luó yī
秋　千　慵　困　解　羅　衣，

huà liáng shuāng yàn guī
畫　梁　雙　燕　歸。

# Tipsy in the Land of Peach Blossoms

by Feng Yan-si

When the South Garden is in half spring,
A walk on grasses which have just turned green.
Breeze is gentle,
You can hear Horse neighing.
Plums as beans green,
Willows as brows slim,
Daytime is long,
Butterflies are flying.

Flower dewdrops are heavy,
Plant smokes are low,
Curtains of homes are falling.
Tired and sleepy by swinging,
She unbuttoned her silk clothing,
On painted beams two swallows are homing.

---

* The name of this tune is also called " Ruan Lang Gui " .

# Appreciation

This was a ci-poem which described the state of going sightseeing in the spring. At the beginning the poet wrote about the scenery as a boy tourist passed by. It was particularly beautiful and delightful. The poet utilized still life and dynamic state descriptions, and combined one with the other to make the picturesque scene come to life.

The poet writes that in half spring, an early youth goes sightseeing. The grasses have just turned green. The breeze is gentle. The horse is neighing. On the way, he sees green plums as beans, slim willows as brows. The sun is shining. The daytime seemes longer, butterflies is flying. In his writing the spring is really sunlit and enchanting.

The second part begins to write the morning scene: " Flower dewdrops are heavy, plant smokes low. " Because it is early in the morning, " curtains of homes are falling. " But a girl is swinging at this time. After she has played a while she gets tired and sleepy. She unbuttons her silk dress. Two swallows fly home, dwell on the painted beams. What a leisurely and comfortable painting he draws! The poet writes the poem from still life, such as " Green plums are as beans, slim willows are as brows " , which points out the season too, and " Flower dewdrops are heavy, plant smokes are low " , which are morning scene. He also writes in a dynamic manner such as: " Breeze is gentle, you can hear horse neighing " , " Daytime is long, Butterflies are flying " " On painted beams two swallows are homing. " He writes in the dynamic way in order to serve as a foil to still life. Such description makes it easy to get a lively and smooth artistic effect. That is why the ci-poem expresses extremly vivid picture.

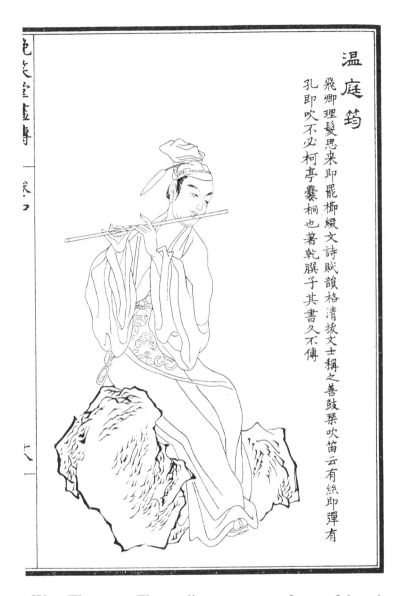

温庭筠

飛卿理髮思来即罷櫛綴文詩賦韻格清拔文士稱之善鼓琴吹笛云有絲即彈有孔即吹不必柯亭爨桐也著乾臊子其書久不傳

Wen Ting-yun : The earliest ancester of graceful and restrained school of ci-poetry

# Sū Mù Zhe
# 蘇幕遮

Fàn Zhòng-yān
范 仲 淹

Bì yún tiān　huáng yè dì
碧 雲 天 ，　黃 葉 地 。

Qiū sè lián bō
秋 色 連 波 ，

bō shàng hán yān cuì
波 上 寒 煙 翠 。

Shān yìng xié yáng tiān jiē shuǐ
山 映 斜 陽 天 接 水 。

Fāng cǎo wú qíng
芳 草 無 情 ，

gèng zài xié yáng wài
更 在 斜 陽 外 。

An xiāng hún　zhuī lǚ sì
黯 鄉 魂 ，　追 旅 思 。

Yè yè chú fēi
夜 夜 除 非 ，

hǎo mèng líu rén shuì
好 夢 留 人 睡 。

Míng yuè lóu gāo xiū dú yǐ
明 月 樓 高 休 獨 倚 ，

Jǐu rù chóu cháng
酒 入 愁 腸 ，

huà zuò xiāng sī lèi
化 作 相 思 淚 。

# Su Mu Zhe

by Fan Zhong-yan


Blue cloudy sky,
Yellow leaves earth,
Autumn scenery reaches the ripples,
Over the ripples cold smokes are emerald.
The setting sun on mountains shimmers,
The sky comes close to the water.
Fragrant grasses have no mercy,
Even stay at the outer
of the setting sun.

My spirit missing the native town,
Overwhelmed by agony,
Lingers the travelling thought.
Night after night,
Unless a nice dream keep me to sleep.
Don't lean alone on the parapet,
Over the high building the moon bright.
Liquor enters the pent-up feelings of sadness,
Will be turned into lovesick teardrops.

# Appreciation

The gist of this ci-poem was leaving with regrets. The first part described the scenery. The first two phrases " Blue cloudy sky, Yellow leaves earth, " pointed out the season. In the clear high sky, the clouds appeared azure blue in the wide open country, yellow leaves covered the earth. These two phrases described from high to low, the typical autumn scenery, and displayed the characteristics of autumn which were boundless, vast, declined and withered. Following these description the poet widened the field of vision. He looked at the distant place and said: " Autumn scenery reaches the ripples, Over the ripples cold smokes are emerald. " Up to the present this ci-poem was writing about the autumn scenery. It stretched long and unbroken, the cold blue smokes shrouded the lake. Here the poet used " ripples " to replace " water " , ripple is more vivid than water. The following sentences " The setting sun on mountains shimmers, The sky comes close to the water " held sky, mountain and river into one line. The setting sun cast light upon the distant mountains, the waves came close to the sky. " The setting sun " referrred to the evening time and the autumn scenery at this time. Up to now, we can say that the poet had written about all the scenery around him. The last two sentences of the first part: " Fragrant grasses have no mercy, Even stay at the outer of the setting sun. " turned to write the thinking of the absent one. The fragrant grasses were boundless, reaching the sky which seemed remoter than the setting sun. In the natural world the green grasses have no emotion. But in ancient poems, poets often used them to express their personal parting emotion. This ci-poem said: the grasses stretched to the remote place far far away, really told us that the poet was reminded of his dear one by them. Saying " no mercy " just reflected the poet's deep emotion. So these two sentences through the description of scenery exposed strong subjective feelings which made a natural transition from describing scenery to expressing emotion in the next part.

The second part expressed: " My spirit missing the native town, Overwhelmed by agony, Lingers the travelling thought. " Thinking of his native town, the poet was overwhelmed by grief. His mood was gloomy. This mood lingered as a traveling thought. Because of this, "night after night" he was unable to sleep. "Unless a nice dream keep me to sleep". In fact, fine dreams were few, especially when a person was overwhelmed by grief. Outwardly these two sentences seemed to say that his sorrow had a time to dispel, inwardly, they described that his sorrow lingered in his mind all the time. A writing like this will make the line more heartfelt and tactful. What was his fine dream? The poet did not say. From the content we can see that it refers to returning home. The following sentences said: "Don't lean alone on the parapet, Over the high building the moon was bright". These two sentences have two meanings. The first one, continued from "Night after night". Every night he was unable to sleep. Though the moonlight was bright, and the night scene on the high building was beautiful, he could not enjoy it because if he leaned alone on the parapet looking into the distance from a high place, he would feel still more distracted, the second part, retrieved the first part contrary, made it clear that all the scenery described was seen by climbing the high building and looking into the distance. Don't lean on the parapet only not to add the sorrow at most, but unable to remove the sorrow. In order to remove the sorrow, the poet drank. So he said: "Liquor entered the pent-up feelings of sadness, will be turned into love sick tear drops." That is to say, the wine entered his stomach, did not remove his sorrow, on the contrary, it became tears, and redoubled his grief.

## A Brief Account of the Author's Life

Fan Zhong-yan (989-1052) styled himself Xi Wen. He was a native of Wu county (now belongs to Jiangsu Province). In 1015 he was a successful candidate in the highest imperial examinations and then became a government official. He was a famous statesman in the Northern Song Dynasty and a main leader in charge of Qin Li New Politics. He was also a famous writer. His works contain "A Collection of Fan Wen Zheng Gong". Only five pieces of his ci-poems were preserved.

# Yǔ Lín Líng
# 雨　霖　鈴

Liǔ Yǒng
柳　永

Hán chán qī qiè
寒　蟬　淒　切，
duì cháng tíng wǎn
對　長　亭　晚，
zhòu yǔ chū xie
驟　雨　初　歇。
Dū mén zhàng yǐn wú xù
都　門　帳　飲　無　緒，
fāng liú liàn chù
方　留　戀　處，
lán zhōu cuī fa
蘭　舟　催　發。
Zhí shǒu xiāng kàn lèi yǎn
執　手　相　看　淚　眼，
jìng wú yǔ níng yè
竟　無　語　凝　噎。
Niàn qù qù qiān lǐ yān bō
念　去　去，千　里　煙　波，
mù ǎi chén chén chǔ tiān kuò
暮　靄　沉　沉　楚　天　闊。

# Bells Ringing in the Coutinuous Heavy Rain

by Liu Yong


Cold cicadas cried sadly,
Towards the long pavalion the sun set,
Heavy shower has just past.
In the camp of Du Men we drank but without mood,
As we couldn't bear to part,
The boatman asked to start.
Holding hands we looked at each other.
Tears falling hard.
Unexpectedly we were without words but choked.
Bearing in mind that you will go(to),
Thousand of li river covered mist,
Falling dusk will be deep,
The sky of Chu is broad.

Duō qíng zì gǔ shāng lí bié
多　情　自　古　傷　離　別，

gèng nǎ kān　lěng luō qīng qiū jié
更　那　堪，冷　落　清　秋　節。

Jīn xiāo jiǔ xǐng hé chù
今　宵　酒　醒　何　處？

Yáng liǔ àn　xiǎo fēng cán yuè
楊　柳　岸，曉　風　殘　月。

Cǐ qù jīng nián
此　去　經　年，

yīng shì liáng chén hǎo jǐng xū shè
應　是　良　辰　好　景　虛　設。

Biàn zōng yǒu
便　縱　有，

qīan zhǒng fēng qíng
千　種　風　情，

gèng yú hé rén shuō
更　與　何　人　說？

Since ancient times the full affectionate has grieved at parting,

How can one still bear the desolate in the Mid-autumn Festival?

Tonight where will you dispel the effects of alcohol?

Poplar and willow bank with a wind at dawn and the moon pitiful.

You will go for years,

From now on,

Beautiful sceneries on bright days should be nominal.

Even if there are thousand types of feelings amorous,

Whom shall I talk?

# Appreciation

This ci-poem wrote parting emotion. One may well say that it was incisive and vivid. The first three sentences pointed out the time, place and scenery. The man would soon leave. The sun was late. A heavy shower has just past. The cicadas cried mournfully. As the sun set, towards a long parting pavalion, how could one endure such cirumstances. The cicadas crying added the grief. At the very beginning the poet included this sound in order to pitch the tune for the whole poem. The following three sentences explained the mood when the poet was giving a farewell dinner: mild and round about, willing to drink but without mood, desiring to stay but in vain. Then the boatman asked to start. " Holding hands we looked each other, tears falling hard. Unexpectedly we were without words but choked. " described the parting men. These three groups of sentences, circled round, paused and transited in rhythm, and cadenced to the utmost. From " Bearing in mind that you will go " to the end of this part, the words flowed forth vigorously, stating the poet's view frankly but deeply. The word " bearing " expressed what the poet imagined after parting. He thought that his friend's journey was: " Thousand of li river covered mist, Falling dusk will be deep. The sky of Chu is broad. " Though all were scenery, the poet cherished a deep tenderness and love.

The next part also began with the word " affectionate ". The poet sighed out that " Since ancient times the full of affectionate has grieved at parting ". He even pushed on a step further. " How can one still bear the desolate in the Mid-autumn Festival? ". The following sentences: " Where will you dispel the effects of alcohol? Poplar and willow bank with a wind at dawn and the moon pitiful. " still were imagination. But the scenery was very quiet and beautiful. The man who was going seemed really to see the bank of poplar and willow, the setting moon and the wind at dawn. The reader could also forget that they were merely an imagination. The last three sentences were also guesses. The poet guessed after parting there would be permanent lonesomeness, he would spend lonely days. " Even if there were a thousand types of feelings amorous, Whom shall I talk? " all would be but an empty shell. The idea! There was still endless regret and the poem left a lasting and pleasant after taste to us.

# Shào Nián Yóu
# 少年遊

## Liǔ Yǒng
## 柳永

Cháng ān gǔ dào mǎ chí chí
長　安　古　道　馬　遲　遲，

gāo liǔ luàn chán si
高　柳　亂　蟬　嘶。

Xī yáng niǎo wài
夕　陽　鳥　外，*

qiū fēng yuán shàng
秋　風　原　上，

mù duàn sì tiān chuí
目　斷　四　天　垂。

Guī yún yī qù wú zōng jí
歸　雲　一　去　無　蹤　跡，

hé chù shì qián qī
何　處　是　前　期？

Xiá xìng shēng shū
狎　興　生　疏，

jiǔ tú xiāo suǒ
酒　徒　蕭　索，

bù shì shào nián shì
不　似　少　年　時。

# Early Youth Wanders

by Liu Yong

On the ancient Changan Road,
The horse walks slow.
In the tall willow,
Cicadas neigh turmoil(ed),
The setting sun is beyond birds.
On grassland blows autumn wind,
My eyesight breaks off,
On the four sides of the sky vast.

Returing clouds have gone without leaving a trace,
Where is the former date?
The interest
of being improperly familiar with others is rusty,
Wine bibbers are desolate,
Unlike my early days.

---

\* The third line of the first part of this tune may be " oblique 仄 oblique 仄 level 平 level 平 " which is the same as the third line of the second part.

# Appreciation

Liu Yong did not achieve all his ambition in life. He wrote his bitter experience into ci-poem. This one is a representative. This ci-poem wrote about autumn scenery at first. In sentiment and sound, it had distinguishing features. In his early days, Liu Yong madly clung(to) and was sentimentally attached to the youthful world, but when he was old, the emotion died away and he also lost interest in advancing triumphantly. This ci-poem is filled with low spirit, desolated tone and sound as a result of that influence.

At the beginning the poet brought up the word " Chang An " . It was an ancient and famous capital. Whenever a poet writes about this city, the heavy traffic on its road often gives the reader a picture of scrambling for fame and high position. But Liu Yong did not mean that. He said: " The horse walks slow " . This sentence just served as a foil to the scramble. He put " ancient " before " road " , in order to make an impression on the readers that the heavy traffic was in an ancient time, not now, and developed all sorts of feelings on many vicissitudes of life.

The second sentence said: " In the tall willow, Cicadas neigh turmoiled " . Originally cicadas crying in autumn have a dreary sentimentalism. Liu Yong used the word " turmoiled " which not only expressed " many " but told us that his mind was very complicated. " The setting sun is beyond birds " drew a picture, that is. when the sun set, it gradually disappeared beyond birds and the countryside was boundless. As the day was waning, on the outskirts the cold wind blew. The sentence " Autumn wind blows on grassland " described that. Where was his home to return to? The sky was dark, the countryside was endless. The poet's eyes looked as far as they could, but he could not find a place for shelter. How desolated his heart was! In the first part, the poet wrote about his own wandering life, hopeless and disappointed, from the scenery of the external world to the internal part of his heart, and sighed with emotion deeply.

The next part began to recall the past. It would be hard for all the hope and happiness to come again. So Liu Yong said: " Returning clouds have gone without leaving a trace. " All events in the world just like the clouds would change, disappear and never return. The clouds were merely metaphors. The poet, describing the clouds, could best express his state of mind. The next sentence said: " Where is the former date? " " The former date " may be explained as his former ambition, or the date with his lover. In a word, it was his wish and expectation. But to Liu Yong, these two had all been lost when he wrote the ci-poem. So he said: " The interest of being improperly familiar with others is rusty, Wine bibbers are desolate, unlike my early days. " Though in his early days he was disappointed, he had lovers and friends. Now they all were old, and accomplished nothing. They idled away their time. He was overcome with grief.

In this poem the scene and emotion supplemented each other. False and true echoed each other too. It was a very good poem which could express Liu Yong's tragic life. His artistic attainments were very high.

## A Brief Account of the Author's Life

Liu Yong(984-1053), styled himself Shi Qin. He was named Shan Bian at first. He was a native of Cong-an, Fujiang Province. He was the first one who wrote a large number of slow ci-poem and made a great contirbution to the development of ci-poetry. His social stratus was frustrated. Until 1034, when he was about 50, he just passed the highest imperial examination and became a successful candidate. He died in Run Zhou (now Jiangsu Province, Zhen Jiang County). His works have " A Collection of Yue Zhang " .

# Huàn Xī Shā
# 浣　溪　沙

Yàn Shú
晏　殊

Yī qǔ xīn cí jiǔ yī bēi
一 曲 新 詞 酒 一 杯，

qù nián tiān qì jiù tíng tái
去 年 天 氣 舊 亭 台，

xī yáng xī xià jǐ shì huì
夕 陽 西 下 幾 時 回？

Wú kě nài hé huā luò qù
無 可 奈 何 花 落 去，

shì céng xiāng shí yàn guī lái
似 曾 相 識 燕 歸 來。

Xiǎo yuán xiāng jìng dú pái huái
小 園 香 徑 獨 徘 徊。

# Washing Sand in the Stream

by Yan Shu


I write a tune of a new poem,
With a cup of wine,
Last year's climate,
And former steps and pavilion.
When will the setting sun headed west return?

Having no choice,
Flowers die.
Swallows' coming back,
I still seem to recognize.
In the small garden,
On the fragrant path,
Up and down alone I pace.

# Appreciation

This ci-poem was clear and simple, but the comprehension of the content was different. In fact it was a poem contemplating an absent lover. Because of the two words " last year ", " climate " " steps and pavilion " and " the setting sun " became the common things of the past and the present. In order to give prominence to the unforgetable sight of the joyful banquet last year, the poet put the sentence " I write a tune of a new poem with a cup of wine " at the beginning of the first part. Among a tune and a tune of new poems, a cup and a cup of fragrant wine, there embodied deep love. The singer's song had been so beautiful that it had appealed to the listener's passionate temperament at that time. However, in late spring, the steps and pavilion where they had met, the setting sun under which they had said goodbye to each other were the same, but the singer had gone. Last year the poet had listened to the song and drunk, and how happy it had been! Today the scene was the same, but where was the singer? Why couldn't the sight strike a chord in his heart? " When will the setting sun headed west return? " expressed the deep feelings that were buried in the poet's heart.

The first part laid stress on writing the thinking of the past, the second part on the sentiment of today. " Having no choice, flowers die, swallows' coming back, I still seem to recognize ". These two sentences in Chinese were two carefully and neatly done sentences, which were a matching of both sound and sense in two lines with matching words in the same part of speech. " Having no choice " meant making every effort but in vain, " seem to recognize " meant seeming to be that but not really that. " Flowers die " and " swallows coming back " were common sights. Once they were written together with " Having no choice " and " seem to recognize ", they became symbols of our familiar things or feelings, not the specific ones. " The flowers die " might stand for spring going so soon or sorry feelings for the happy life dying away. Though " swallows coming back " was a real description of scenery, it might also stand for the thinking of past when one visited the old haunt. Flowers die, things were past. Swallows return to their old nest, where was the singer? All sorts of feelings welled up in the poet's mind. So although these two sentences seemed to write about the scenery, they really contained substantial content. The last sentence " In the small garden, On the fragrant path, Up and down alone I pace. " said that on the old fragrant path where they had walked together hand in hand, the flowers had fallen, so the poet now paced alone and revived the old dream by himself. Reading this poem again from the beginning, we can easily find that listening to the song, drinking, the climate, steps and pavilion, setting sun, the falling flowers and returning swallows all were things seen when he was pacing. The poet really cherished a very deep affection for every thing. Though there was no flowery diction, the poem was evry moving.

## A Brief Account of the Author's Life

Yan Shu (991-1055) styled himself Tong Shu, was a native of Fu Zhou, Liu Chuan (now belongs to Jiangxi Province). After his death, people called him Yan Yuan-xian. When he was very young, he was called to be examined as a child prodigy and was granted a class origin the same as a successful candidate in the highest imperial examinations. He was a government official in Zhen Zong's and Ren Zong's courts. Fan Zhong-yan, Han Qi, Ou-yang Xiu were all his students. He was rich all his life, so his poems described mainly songs, wine, wind and moon which contained a leisurely and carefree mood. He was an important ci-poet in the Northern Song Dynasty ci-poem world. " Pearls and Jades Ci-poems " were his works.

# Yù Lóu Chūn
# 玉 樓 春 *

Sòng Qí
宋 祁


Dōng chéng jiàn jué fēng guāng hǎo
東 城 漸 覺 風 光 好，

hú zhòu bō wén yíng kè zhào
縠 縐 波 紋 迎 客 棹。

Lù yáng yān wài xiǎo hán qīng
綠 楊 煙 外 曉 寒 輕，

hóng xìng zhī tóu chūn yì nào
紅 杏 枝 頭 春 意 鬧。


Fú shēng cháng hèn huān yú shǎo
浮 生 長 恨 歡 娛 少，

kěn ài qiān jīn qīng yī xiào
肯 愛 千 金 輕 一 笑。

Wèi jūn chí jiǔ quàn xié yàng
爲 君 持 酒 勸 斜 陽，

qiě xiàng huā jiān liú wǎn zhào
且 向 花 間 留 晚 照。

# Spring in the Magnificent Pavilion

Song Qi

I gradually find,
That the sight of Dong Cheng is good.
Ripples like crape greet passenger's boat.
Green pillows as smoke are distant,
Dawn cold is light,
On branches red flowers of apricot,
Show that spring is very much about.

In a showy life I always regret,
That happiness is short,
How can I love a thousand pieces of gold,
So much as to treat a sweet laugh without respect.
I want to raise the glass for you,
to urge the setting sun,
to accompany us among flowers a few moment.

---

\* The name of this tune is also called " Mu Lan Hua " (Magnolia).

# Appreciation

This is a famous ci-poem. People take delight in talking about the sentence " On branches the red flowers of apricot show that spring is very much about " . For this reason the poet at that time soon received a good reputation.

The first part wrote of scenery. The first sentence described generally a sunlit and enchanting scene of spring. The second sentence turned to write what is actually happening. On the surface of the water, ripples like crape looked as if they would greet the passenger's boat. This personification skill made the description vivid. The third and fourth sentences wrote from far to near. In the distance, there were green pillows as smoke. Though it was early morning, the cold draught was light. This word " light " with " very much " in the next line, were true qualities of the scenery, but written carefully and cleverly. Then came closer, " On branches the red flowers of apricot " was a feature, showing the tree was in full bloom. The apricot blossoms made spring stand out by contrast. The words " very much " once used, brought the spring realm into sight. It's really a word worth a thousand pieces of gold.

The next part turned writing about scenery into expressing emotion. A showy life was but a dream, causing much suffering and little happiness. How could one love money so much as to give up a great joy in the twinkling of an eye. " I want to raise the glass for you " , here " you " referred to friends who were strolling about with the poet. In order to enjoy themselves to the full, the poet said: " To urge the setting sun, To accompany us among flowers a few moment " . From this sightseeing, the poet and his friends were reluctant to leave. This mood overflowed on the paper. The setting sun is extremly good, but it is near dusk. This might be the poet's thought.

# A Brief Account of the Author's Life

Song Qi (998-1061), styled himself Zi Jing. He was a native of Anzhou, Anlu (now belongs to Hubei Province). Later his family moved to Kaifeng, Yongqiu (now Qi county in Henan Province). In 1024, he became a successful candidate after the highest imperial examinations. Then he was raised to the position of a goverment official until he became a member of the lmperial Academy. He had compiled "New Tang's Book" together with Ou-yang Xiu and so on. After he died, he was given a name Jing Wen. Later generations called him Song Jing Wen Gong. His poems often wrote about individual life. His language was fine, lively and vivid. His works had "Chang Duan Ju of Song Jing Wen Gong"

# Shēng Chá Zǐ
# 生　查　子

Oū-yáng Xiū
歐　陽　修

Qù nián ynán yè shí
去　年　元　夜　時，

huā shì dēng rú zhoù
花　市　燈　如　畫。

Yuè shàng liǔ shāo tóu
月　上　柳　梢　頭，

rén yuē huáng hūn hòu
人　約　黃　昏　後。

Jīn nián yuán yè shí
今　年　元　夜　時，

yuè yú dēng yī jiù
月　與　燈　依　舊。

Bú jiàn qù nián rén
不　見　去　年　人，

lèi shī chūn shān xiù
淚　濕　春　衫　袖。

# Song of Fresh Berries

by Ou-yang Xiu


Last year on the Lunar Festival,
The lanterns in the flower market were,
As bright as daylight.
The moon rose,
To the tip branches of the willow,
After dusk,
I was appointed to meet a fellow.

This year on the Lunar Festival,
The moon and the lanterns are as before.
I do not see the last year fellow,
The sleeves of my spring dress,
Bath in tears.

# Appreciation

Yuan Xi, also called Yuan Ye, is the night of 15th of the 1st lunar month. Since the Tang Dynasty, certain places have been set ablaze with lanterns each Yuan Ye. People are accustomed to going there to look at the lanterns. So the night is a night of jubilation. It is always related with love. This ci-poem is one singing its praises of glorious love by Yuan Ye.

The plot of this ci-poem was ingeniously conceived. It took the skill of contrast of a multi-administrative structure: such as contrasting the present with the past, noisy with quiet and joys with sorrows. One layer was deeper than another, to express the sincere feelings of the heroine's inner heart.

The first part said that the heroine looked back at the secret date with her lover on Yuan Ye last year. The writer used the words " flower market " to describe generally the sight of Yuan Ye, making the time and place of the date clear. Flower market was the market for selling and admiring flowers every spring. Though the day was over, the market still open. Beautiful lanterns were brightly lit which made the market as bright as the day. So we could see how prosperous it was. The sentence " The moon rose to the tip of the branches of the willow " further told us the time of the date. " Moon " and " willow " contrasted finely with each other, which made the date richer in poetic flavour. The moon on the fifteenth is round and bright. It symbolizes the perfect love. Willows in ancient poetry were always used as imageries of love. The branches of willows swayed slightly under the bright and clear moonlight, how many tender feelings would it give to the sweetheart date. This sentence interweaved the three: moon, willow and lovers with each other and constituted a realm of warm and sweet, an unity of happiness.

The second part described the scene of Lantern Festival that year. " The moon and the lanterns are as before " , told us that all the scenery was as last year. These same things foreshadowed the later development of "man changes". The scenery still looked the same but the lover of last year was not at her side, how could she not be disconsolate and miserable. The ci-poem did not tell us why the lover disappeared. There might be something embarrassing to mention. "I do not see the last year fellow" gave the reader ample places to image. Last year the oriole was a companion and the swallow was a partner, but now only herself left alone. The happiness of former days only became the misfortune of today. So the heroine says: "The sleeves of my spring dress, Bath in tears."

## A Brief Account of the Author's Life

Ou-yang Xiu (1007-1072), was a native of Lu Ling (now Jiangxi Province, Ji An county). In 1030, he became a successful candidate in the highest imperial examinations. He worked as government official from county magistrate to a minister of the ministry of war. After that he was selected as the teacher of the crown prince. He was presented with a name of "The Old Teacher of Crown Prince" and after his death, he was respectfully called "Wen Zhong". As he was the county magistrate of Chu county, he styled himself "The Drinker" and nicknamed Liu Yi Lay Buddhist in his later years. His collections left are "Liu Yi Ci-poems" "Folk Songs and Ballads in Modern Style" and "The Drinker's Qin Tastes Extra Editing".

# Mù Lán Huā
# 木 蘭 花*

## Oū-yáng Xiu
## 歐 陽 修

Bié hòu bù zhī jūn yuān jìn
別 後 不 知 君 遠 近，

chù mù qī liáng duō shǎo mèn
觸 目 淒 涼 多 少 悶。

Jiàn xīng jiàn yuǎn jiàn wú shū
漸 行 漸 遠 漸 無 書，

Shuǐ kuò yū chén hé chú wèn
水 闊 魚 沉 何 處 問？

Yè shēn fēng zhú qiāo qiū yùn
夜 深 風 竹 敲 秋 韻，

wàn yè qiān shēng jiē shì hèn
萬 葉 千 聲 皆 是 恨。

Gù qī dān zhěn mèng zhōng xún
故 欹 單 枕 夢 中 尋，

mèng yòu bù chéng dēng yòu jìn
夢 又 不 成 燈 又 燼。

# Magnolia

by Ou-yang Xiu


Since we departed,
I did not know you were far or near.
Whenever I look at,
The desolation I can't bear.
Little by little you travelled,
You were away farther and farther.
Your letters grew fewer,
Broad is the water,
Deep swim the shoals,
Where
Can I ask for your mail?


The wind and bamboos knock the autumn rhyme
at the dead of night.
Myriad leaves and thousand sounds are all regrets.
I recline on the solitary pillow wilfully in search
of dreams,
But dreams do not come while guttering out is
the lamp.

---

*The name of this tune is also called "Yu Lou Chun", but the first line "⊙ oblique(仄) ⊙ level(平) level(平) oblique(仄) oblique(仄)" is different from the first line of Song Qi's "Yu Lou Chun" which is "⊙ level(平) ⊙ oblique(仄) level(平) level(平) oblique(仄)". People in Song Dynasty, often followed Song Qi's style.

# Appreciation

There are many poems of past narrated sorrow for leaving or the regret of parting. This Magnolia by Ou-yang Xiu had a unique style with his own distinguished features.

This ci-poem described a woman's deep and miserable regret from separation. The first and second parts wrote about her desolation and gloom after the separation from her lover. The first part was written extensively, the second, concretely. In composition and means of artistic expression the poet showed ingenuity and excellent artistic wrist strength.

At the beginning of the ci-poem the writer pointed out the time "After the parting". The readers know at the first sight that this was a ci-poem telling of a separation situation. But "I did not know you were far or near" was a sentence which seemed common yet rugged. How could a wife not know where her husband went while he was going on a tour? It looked as if there was something embarrassing to mention, so the poet couldn't conveniently say. Thus she continued "Wherever I look at, the desolation I can't bear." The third sentence was another magnificent peak tower. "Little by little you travelled, You were away farther and farther. Your letters grew fewer." This sentence interweaved the woman's guess with the hard fact. The foregoing sentence said: "I did not know you were far on near", yet says here: "you were away farther and farther. They seemed to be contradictory. Why? Examine carefully and we can understand that the woman received fewer and fewer letters till not even one. She was obliged to guess that her lover was farther and farther away. His letters growing fewer did not mean something to worry about (such as loving the new and loathing the old). Just because he was far away from home, the letters were hard to reach her. Such a sentence portrayed the woman's contradictory, complicated and minute activities in her heart deeply and clearly. In ancient China, it was said that the fish and wild goose could deliver letters. The following sentences sourced from this legend. " The water is broad, the shoals swim deep ", she wanted to ask why she couldn't get a letter, but she was not able to find a fish. " Where can I ask for your mail? " told us her indescribable distress.

The second part depicted the woman's life from day to the deep of night, choosing a particular and typical autumn night. This part further described the woman's agony of lovesickness. During the day, " Wherever I look at I can't bear the desolation ", how did she feel at nights? " The wind and bamboos knock the autumn rhyme ". These were beautiful sounds that people loved to hear. Since she was deeply grieved, those sounds were not to her liking but as someone accused while weeping, making her more worried.

" Myriad leaves and thousand sounds are all regrets. " This sentence told us that every sound around her seemed to deliver regret. From full of grieves in her mind to full of regret in her heart, the heroine under the writer's pen really had no way out. Up to the present, the ci-poem might be ended. But the writer did not stop, he just changed his tip of pen. When she was filled with despair, he gave her a gleam of hope at first. The ci-poem said: " I recline on the solitary pillow wilfully in search of dream ". Though dream was unreal, it might relieve the feelings of sadness a little. But soon this pitiful hope was dashed too. The last sentence said: " But dreams do not come while guttering out is the lamp. " One on a solitary pillow had already not been the right flavour. If there was a lamp, it would bring some warm to her, but now it was also guttering out. Before the heroine's and readers' eyes, only dark mass was left.

# Dié Liàn Huā
# 蝶　戀　花

Oū-yáng Xiū
歐　陽　修


Tíng yuàn shēn shēn shēn jǐ xǔ
庭　院　深　深　深　幾　許？

Yáng lǐu duī yān, lián mù wú chóng shǔ
楊　柳　堆　煙　簾　幕　無　重　數。

Yù lè diāo ān yóu yě chù
玉　勒　雕　鞍　游　冶　處，

lóu gāo bú jiàn zhāng tái lù
樓　高　不　見　章　台　路。


Yǔ héng fēng kuáng sān yuè mù
雨　橫　風　狂　三　月　暮，

mén yǎn huáng hūn, wú jì líu chūn zhù
門　掩　黃　昏　無　計　留　春　住。

Lèi yǎn wèn huā huā bù yǔ
淚　眼　問　花　花　不　語，

luàn hóng feī huò qīu qiān qù
亂　紅　飛　過　鞦　韆　去。


116

# Butterflies Love Flowers

by Ouyang Xiu


The courtyard is deep and deep,
How deep will it be?
Clusters of willows are like mist heaps,
Curtains, layer upon layer, can't be counted.
Son of a high official,
Rides on jade rein and carved saddle,
Strolling about the brothel.
Though my building is so high,
I don't see the Zhang Tai Trail.

The wind blows hard,
And the rain comes down in sheets.
It's late March.
I close the door,
The dusk is covered.
I am at my wits' end,
To keep the spring not from leaving.
With tearful eyes I ask,
But the flowers do not reply.
Disorderly the red petals are floating,
Over the swing of the court.

# Appreciation

This ci-poem exquisitely describes the distressed mood of a lady in her boudoir in the feudal society.

At the beginning of the first part, the poet portrays a typical circumstance for the woman. There are three " deeps " in the first sentence which vigorously describes the depth and serenity of the court yard where the woman lives. " How " is a word of rough estimate which means a certain number. Here the poet uses interrogative mood in order to emphasize the degree of " deep " and to form a delightful contrast with the following sentences: " Clusters of willows are like mist heaps, Curtains, layer upon layer, can' t be counted ". The description of willow and curtain means: the willows gathered together closely look like the smoke piled up, and also like curtains, layer upon layer, that can' t be counted. These willows make inside and outside separate. Originally the courtyard was deep, now seems deeper. The heroine if lives in such a deep but richly decorated jade palace, ought not to have known how to worry; but when she has decked herself out and reached the high building, she is in no mood to enjoy the excellent spring scenery. She has her heart filled with worry. She looks at a distant place, where her husband wallowed in. The jade rein and carved saddle refers to the son of high officials' horse which wear horse gear made of jade and a saddle decorated with carved flowers. Those sons are men always inconstant in love. They seek pleasure in the brothel, in what is called the Zhang Tai Trail. Through the description the distressed mood of a noble lady who lives in a deep boudoir is shown in the writing. " Jade rein " describes the pleasure of the fickle husband,
" did not see " refers to the lady's sadness. The lady and her husband two sides are a striking contrast. Besides, the beginning three sentences tells us that the lady's residence is a comfortable magnificent high building and deep court yard. The lady who lives in such a place ought to find the scenery pleasing to both the eye and the mind. On the contrary, she is very sad. Here the poet uses happy scene to express a worry, redoubles the sadness.

The next part points out the time which is late March. " The wind blows hard and the rain come down in sheets. " describes the character of the climate. The spring is late, which already makes one unable to bear, let alone the wind blowing hard and the rain coming down in sheets, which hastens the spring's fading away. And still it is a time near dusk. These three things duplicates the sadness. A layer was deeper than a deeper layer, causes the readers to be overcome with grief. So she has to close the door and keeps herself in an empty room alone. She said: " I am at my wit's end to keep the spring not from leaving " In this sentence, ' spring ' has profound implications. First, it might refer to spring; second, to glorious youth, third, love. This is really a soul-stirring word. It describes the heroine's inner world deeply and exquisitely.

The concluding sentences says: " With tearful eyes I ask, but the flowers do not reply. The red petals are floating disorderly over the swing. " These two sentences are famous lines always admired. Because of the flowers, she sheds tears, this is the first implication; owing to the tears, she asks the flowers, this is the second; but the flowers do not answer, is the third; They are falling and flying disorderly over the swing the fourth. The more she grieves, the more annoying are the flowers. Though these words are plain, the meaning is very deep. You are unable to see the mark of great effort. It is really flawless. The flowers are given a person's thought and feelings by personification skill. The lady's tearful eyes see them and ask them, they do not answer, but is floating one after another over the swing. Could we say: the lady pines for love while the heartless flowers do not requite her? Or say the lady and the flowers have the same miserable lot? The poet uses the flowers falling and flying over the swing to hint that the lady has no one to depend on. Though he does not say clearly, he leaves it to the readers. We feel that these sentences have a special pleasing quality about them.

# Làng Táo Shā Lìng
# 浪　淘　沙　令

Wáng An-shí
王　安　石

Yī Lǚ liǎng shuāi wēng
伊　呂　兩　衰　翁，

lì biàn qióng tōng
歷　遍　窮　通，

yī wéi diào sǒu yī gēng yóng
一　爲　釣　叟　一　耕　傭。

Ruò shǐ dāng shí shēn bú yù
若　使　當　時　身　不　遇，

lǎo liǎo yīng xióng
老　了　英　雄。

Tāng　Wǔ oǔ xiāng féng
湯　武　偶　相　逢，

fēng hǔ yún lóng
風　虎　雲　龍，

xīng wáng zhǐ zài xiào tán zhōng
興　亡　只　在　笑　談　中。

Zhí zhì rú jīn qiān zǎi hòu
直　至　如　今　千　載　後，

shúi yú zhēng gōng
誰　與　爭　功？

# Song of Waves Washing Sands

by Wang An-shi

Yi Yin and Lu Shang, two old and feeble men,
Had gone through all kinds of impoverishment,
But held sensible views.
One was a fisherman,
The other cultivated the land.
If at that time they had not got the opportunities,
The two heroes would have been old in vain.

Chen Tang and Wu Wang met them by chance,
As the wind follows a tiger,
And the clouds follow a dragon.
What prospered the nation was advanced,
Only during talking cheerfully.
Up to now a thousand years have passed,
Who would compete for credit with them?

# Appreciation

This is a ci-poem narrating history. It refers to the life of Yi Yin and Lu Shang.

Yi Yin was a slave originally. Because of his remarkable ability he was spotted by Chen Tang. Chen Tang appointed him to assist with national affairs. He helped him eliminate the Xia Dynasty of Jie and fostered the Shang Dynasty. After Chen Tang's death, Yi Yin still assisted the two succeeding emperors in governing the country and consolidating the Shang regime.

Lu Shang Was also called Jiang Tai Gong . He was poor in his early years. He went angling on the Weihe and Jin River in old age. On the bank he met Zhou Wen Wang. Later he assisted Wu Wang in governing the country and accomplished the great cause of elimintaing Zhou (紂) and fostering the Zhou Dynasty. Yi Yin and Lu Shang were famous worthy prime ministers. For bringing talent into play and accomplishing a deed, besides outstanding ability, circumstances and conditions are still more important. Since ancient times, how many persons of outstanding ability were stifled? Compared with them, Yi Yin and Lu Shang were very Lucky. So the writer says: " If at that time they had not got the opportunities, the two heroes would have been old in vain. " It is clear that the writer has dual ideas. First he advocates taking an active part into the affairs of human life which is different from the disciples of Lao Zhuang who loved leisure and a carefree life. Second he points out that whether a great task can be accomplished has a certain contingency. The times produces their heroes. Without a certain background of times and the opportunity, nothing can be done.

In regard to official career, the writer forges ahead sparing no effort. He is brimming with warmth towards political deeds. So in the second part, his feeling is aroused. He says: " Chen Tang and Wu Wang met them by chance, As the wind follows a tiger and the clouds follow a dragon. What prospered the nation was advanced only during talking cheerfully. " Then Dynasties changed, states were founded. They performed outstanding services. The prosperity of the nation advanced only during cheerfully talking. Time brought great changes to the world. In the poetic writings, to be a builder of a nation seems relaxed and leisurely. This expresses that Wang Anshi respects his predecessors a lot. After that it is evident that he encourages himself deeply. " Up to now a thousand years have passed, Who would compete for credit with them? " This sentence means: after thousand years, today, outwardly, their contributions are immortal, nobody could compete with them; inwardly the writer is rather conceited. Though the causes of Yi and Lu were matchless through the ages, who could be truly great men? We should see the present. The writer in fact claims to be equal to Yi and Lu. His political aspiration can be seen from the last sentence which expresses doubt about their achievements.

This ci-poem has strong practical significance and political colour. It has shaken off the purely decorative aid in ci-poems and can be regarded as an important work in the history of the development of the ci-poem in its boldness and lack of constraint.

# A Brief Account of the Author's Life

Wang An-shi (1021-1086) styled himself Jie Fu. In his later years he assumed a name Ban Shan. He was a native of Fu Zhou Lin Chuan (now Jiangxi Province). In 1042, he became a successful candidate in the highest imperial examinations. During the years of Shen Zong Xi Ning of the Song Dynasty he was twice prime minister and put his political reforms into practice. He attempted to change the poor and weak face of his country. After his death he was named " Wen ". He was sent a respectful form of address: " Tai Shi " . During the years of Chong Ning, he was offered subsequently " Shu Wang " . His works include " A collection of Wang Wen Gong ". Only about twenty pieces of his ci-poems are left.

# Shēng Chá Zǐ
# 生　查子

Yàn Jǐ-dào
晏　幾　道

Duò yǔ yǐ cí yún
墮雨已辭雲，

líu shuǐ nán guī pǔ
流水　難歸浦。

Yí hèn jǐ shí xīu
遺恨　幾時休？

Xīn dǐ qīu lián kǔ
心　抵秋蓮苦。


Rěn lèi bù něng gē
忍　淚不　能　歌，

shì tuō āi xián yǔ
試托哀弦語。

Xián yǔ yuàn xiāng féng
弦語　愿　相　逢，

zhī yǒu xiāng féng fǒu
知有　相　逢否？

# Song of Fresh Berries

by Yan Ji-dao

The falling rain has already left clouds,
It is hard for running water to return to the
river mouth.
When will the eternal regret have paused?
The bitterness of the heart is equal to that of autumn
lotus.

Tears have endured so that I couldn't sing,
In order to speak I tried to rely on the sad string.
It says: " Meeting is the will of Heaven. "
Do you know if we will meet again?

# Appreciation

This ci-poem describes a lady's agony of disappointment in a love affair. Judged by the agonies of pain, the lady might have been passionately in love with her sweetheart. Her result is corresponding deep. But the poet does not write this. He only cuts a cross-section and concentrates on portraying the heroine's feelings after her disappointment. The first two sentences uses two bright metaphors successively to express that their love could not be rehabilitated. Then the fourth sentence utilizes the autumn lotus to explain that she is in a painful frame of mind. Anticipating this, the third sentence uses a question to ask: "When will the eternal regret have paused?" The tone suddenly rises, which makes the readers seem to hear her sigh. The tone of its answer abruptly becomes lower and deeper, which makes the readers seem to hear her moan and groan. In this rising and falling melody the lady's grief is carefully and lively described.

The second part continues closely from the preceding part. It says that she wants to give vent to her personal feelings by singing a song, but she doesn't open her mouth, tears starts from her eyes. The word "endure" depicts her disposition and manner. When she suffers disappointment in love, she is not downcast, but restrains her passion as far as possible and tries hard to brace up. Though her voice isn't pleasing, she tries to rely on the sad string. The melodious Qin sound seems to give her some consolation. The last but one sentence writes: "Meeting is the will of Heaven." But that is an illusion, idiotic nonsense, which reflects that she still has a gleam of a dream in her heart of hearts though her lover is really very inconstant in love. Here the writer brings to light a good but unbending heart. The last sentence: "Do you konw if we will meet again?" is another transition. It describes the heroine's clear-headed yet perplexed contradictory heart. This ci poem ends with a question. It leaves a question mark in the readers' hearts too, which gives them much food for thought.

# A Brief Account of the Author's Life

Yan Ji-dao (1048-1113) styled himself Shu Yuan, Xiao Shan was his assumed name. He was the seventh son of Yan Shu. He came from an official's family but he refused to play up to people of power and influence. He had a proud and aloof temperament so his official career was full of frustration. His highest position was only a Tui Guan of the Perfecture of Kaifen. Because he suffered defeat he tasted to the full the bitterness of life. He often wrote of joys and sorrows, partings and reunions—vicissitudes of life, exceedingly sentimental, miserable and moving. His works has something in " Xiao Shan Ci-poems " and others.

# Sī Yuǎn Rén
# 思　遠　人

Yàn Jǐ-dào
晏　幾　道

Hóng yè huáng huā qiū yì wǎn
紅　葉　黃　花　秋　意　晚，

qiān lǐ niǎn xíng kè
千　里　念＊行　客。

Feī yún gùo jìn, guī hóng wú xìn
飛　雲　過　盡　歸　鴻　無　信，

hé chù jǐ shū dé
何　處　寄＊書　得。

Lèi tán bú jìn lín chuāng di
淚　彈　不　盡　臨　窗　滴，

jiù yàn xuǎn yán mò
就　硯　旋＊研　墨。

Jiàn xǐe dào bíe lái
漸　寫　到　別　來，

cǐ qíng shēn chù
此　情　深　處，

hóng jiān wěi wú sè
紅　箋　爲＊無　色。

# Thinking of a Remote One

by Yan Ji-dao

Red leaves and chrysanthemun show autumn to be late.
I long for the traveller a thousand li away.
Flying clouds have flown past,
Returning swan geese bring no words,
Where will my letter be sent ?

Forth endlessly tears spring,
Just before the window dripping.
With them on an inkslab
I immediately rub a stick of ink.
Little by little,
I write of the time to part.
Of the depth of the love,
The red letter paper loses its colour.

---

\* The four words, 念 nian, 寄 ji, 旋 xuan, 爲 wei, all read the third tone.
(According to 《 The rules of Ci-poems 》of Wan Shu)

# Appreciation

This is a ci-poem which describes a woman thinking of a lover far away. The first sentence, " Red leaves and chrysanthemun show autumn to be late " draws a special picture of late autumn and reveals the sorrowful tone of it. The flowers and grasses will soon wither in autumn. The wind is soughing, the moonlight is cool. All this entice one into thinking of a remote lover. So the second sentence says: " I long for the traveller a thousand li away. " Flying clouds in the sky drifted from place to place. They looked like the dear one travelling far away. Now they had flown past, scattered and disappeared. The returning swans, outside the clouds, ought to have brought home consoling information. But no word came. The letters were obstructed. The heroine wanted to communicate with her lover, where would her letter be sent? It seems she is at the end of her rope. But the most difficult thing in the world is to end a love, the most unreasoning thing is the passion. Though there seems no hope at all, the woman's love can't be refrained and cut off. So the separating sorrow becomes sad tears. She even dripes her tears before the window. Why? She often stands there to see the horizen, the remotest place, whether her lover will appear. The tears drip into an inkslab, with them she immediately rubs an inkstick, using the tears and ink to write. The more the tears, the more bitter the separating sorrow. In the ink the lovesickness was deep. In describing the figure's action and psychology, her wretched and infatuated mind is written to the utmost. The third sentence of the second part says: " Little by litte I write to the time to part " . Here the poet touches her to the very saddest place. Because the deeper the love, the sadder the feelings of departure. The tears of the heroine fall like spring. But the poet does not use the word " tears " . He just says: " The red letter paper loses its colour " . Why " to the depth of the love " , " the letter paper loses ito colour " ? Originally, the love, whether deep or shallow, can't influence the colour of the letter paper. The reason why the paper is bound to lose its colour is that her tears drench it, which make the colour fade away. However, we can faintly see: though the

colour has lost, the love is deep. This ci poem writes " tears " .
" lovesickness " etc. These are all common phenomena. But
" with tears. . . rub an ink stick on an inkslab " and using them to
" write " are the writer's strange thought. He does not say the
tears drench the paper, but says " to the depth of the love " ,
" the red letter paper loses its colour " . His workmanship has been
even more wonderful, excelling nature.

# Bū Shuàn Zǐ
## 卜 算 子

Wáng Guàn
王　觀

Shuǐ shì yǎn bō héng
水 是 眼 波 橫,
shān shì méi fēng jù
山 是 眉 峰 聚。
Yù wèn xíng rén qù nǎ biān
欲 問 行 人 去 那 邊?
Méi yǎn yíng yíng chù
眉 眼 盈 盈 處。

Cái shǐ sòng chūn guī
才 始 送 春 歸,
yòu sòng jūn guī qù
又 送 君 歸 去。
Ruò dào jiāng dōng gǎn shàng chūn
若 到 江 東 趕 上 春,
qiān wàn hé chūn zhù
千 萬 和 春 住。

# Song of Divination

by Wang Guan


Water is just like eye waves transverse,
Mountains are brow peaks knitted.
If you ask where will the pedestrian go?
The place eyes and brows are limpid.

I have just seen spring off,
Then have to see your way home.
If you arrive Jiang Dong,
And catch up with spring,
Be sure to stop with him.

# Appreciation

The author's friend, Bao Hao-ran went to the eastern part of Zhe Jiang(province). He saw Bao off and wrote this poem affectionately with a strange idea. The first part wrote his traveling route through mountains and rivers which expresses the author's deep feelings reluctant to part. The second part states his views frankly and his wishes to his friend. In ancient times " the eyebrow was often likened to the spring mountain ", " the eye to the autumn river ". But the first two sentences adopts an original approach sedulously reconditioned. First, the poet did not use wave and peaks to describe beautiful girl's eyes and eyebrows, which were often used in this way before, but used them to describe his own eyes and eyebrows. Second, conversely he said water was eye waves and mountains were brow peaks. He transformed scenery description into emotion description, changed the natural mountain and water into something affectionate. The poet's friend went further and further, his line of sight and appearance followed his friend on end, which showed his deep love.

" Eyewaves transverse " means his eyes filled with tears, " brow peaks knitted " means his brows locked. His association, figure of speech and description are very lively and vivid. The third and fourth sentences, " If you ask where will the pedestrian go? The place eyes and brows are limpid. " are sentences with double meanings. The plot of the ci-poem is gorgeously beautiful. " Eyes and brows are limpid " both describes the place where his friend would go and the facial expression when he saw his friend off. The implicit meaning is wonderful.

The first two sentences of the second part, " I have just seen spring off, then have to see your way home. " states the parting directly. Spring has returned. It was at the poet's wits' end. Only this already made him unbearable. Now his friend would advance south. The parting was near at hand. How was he to handle the matter? The poem uses " just see " and " then have to see... " to describe the poet's overwhelmed sorrow which is very profound. The writer is a native of Ru Gao county, which is near the Yangtze River.

He wanted to return but could not. It is easy to image how deep his own grief was. He constrained it, but said: " If you arrive Jiang Dong and catch up with spring, be sure to stop with him. " Those words expresses that he valued spring highly and entrusted this hope to his friend. What does it mean? He had lost both spring and his friend. Being economical of spring, he really entertained a hate to see his friend off. He wished his friend would stop with spring. This was a good wish but couldn't be realized. The poet did not write mournful view but put forward an idle dream, in practice, he was in greater distress. He created a style all his own.

## A Brief Account of the Author's Life

Wang Guan styled himself Tong Sou. He is a native of Ru Gao. Nobody knows when he was born and died. In 1057, he was a successful candidate in the highest imperial examinations. He was once a county magistrate of Jiangdu. His highest position was a member of the imperial academy. Because Gao empress dowager thought one of his poem treating Sheng Zong without proper respect, he was dismissed from the office. He had been proclaimed himself " a guest ordered to leave " ever since. His works " A collection of Guan Liu ", was already lost, with only sixteen pieces of the ci-poems still in existence.

# Bū Shuàn Zǐ
# 卜 算 子

Sū Shì
蘇軾

Quē yùe guà shū tóng
缺 月 掛 疏 桐，
lòu duàn rén chū jìng
漏 斷 人 初 靜。
Shúi jiàn yōu rén dú wǎng lái
誰 見 幽 人 獨 往 來？
Piāo miǎo gū hóng yǐng
縹 緲 孤 鴻 影。

Jīng qī quē húi tóu
驚 起 卻 回 頭，
yǒu hèn wú rén xīng
有 恨 無 人 省。
Jiǎn jìn hán zhī bù kěn qī
揀 盡 寒 枝 不 肯 棲，
jī mò shā zhōu lěng
寂 寞 沙 洲 冷。

# Song of Divination

by Su Shi


Crescent moon hangs on sparse Paulownia tree.
The night is waning and people has just sleep.
Who sees
The secluded man coming and going alone?
Only the dimly discernible shadow of the solitary
swan goose.

It startles and still turns round,
Nurses hatred in heart but no one knows,
Selects all the cold branches yet is not willing to stay,
The lonely shoal is frosty.

# Appreciation

This ci-poem was done in December 1082 when the writer was banished to Huang Zhou. It was magnificently conceived. The meaning of the words was noble and splendid. At that time the poet did not yet recovered from the fright, his heart still fluttering with fear. This ci-poem mirrored his lonely psychology.

The first two sentences of the first part, " Crescent moon hangs on sparse Paulownia tree. The night is waning and people has just sleep " arranges an envirronment for " the secluded man " and " the solitary swan goose " " coming and going alone " , which give the reader a very quiet state. The distinguish feature of this circumstance is " just silent " and " the dim light " , which describes his frame of mind. Because his business ventures struck out, he felt the land was boundless but he had no place to stay. He wrote: " Who sees the secluded man coming and going alone? Only the dimly discernible shadow of the solitary swan goose. " He was very lonely.

The second part concentrates in describing the swan goose, which hinted obliquely at himself. Why " the swan startles and still turns round " ? The reason it stayed but not settled was " it nurses hatred in heart but no one knows " . How could a swan goose hate? The writer thought so. Thus it could be seen that the hate was really the writer's which was concealed deeply. The swan goose did not dwell on wood but on reed. This was its habits. The ci-poem goes; " Selects all the cold branches yet not willing to stay " , this description seems to be incorrect. In fact, here the poet pleaded for expressing his own thought. No one compelled a swan goose to dwell on reed. It was just willing to do so. One could well perceive its character and morals. This was really the writer's. The colder the lonely shoal, the firmer the writer.

To sum up: the first part writes of the man, yet we could see the swan goose there. The second part writes of the swan goose but really the man. Between the man and the swan goose, there seemed no gap. The idea which the writer pleaded for is thus: the man was like the swan goose; the swan goose was like the man. Not the man and not the swan goose were the very man and the very swan goose. This was the distinguishing feature of this artistic figure the writer gave us in this ci-poem. This is his artistic style.

## A Brief Account of the Author's Life

Su Shi(1037-1101), styled himself Zi Zhan, or He Zhong. He alternatively named himself Dong Po Lay Buddhist. He is a native of Mei Shan(now a county of Si Chuan Province). His father was Su Xun, brother Su Zhe. They three were equally called three Sues in literary history. When he was only twenty two, he became a successful candidate in the highest imperial examinations. The chief examiner, Ou-yang Xiu appreciated his talent very much. Su Shi submitted a written statement to the emperor and asked to reform politics of that time. But when Wang An-shi carried out political reform, he merely saw some of its corrupt practices and wrote to the emperor to fight against it. So, in the years of Yuan Feng, he was accused of satirizing new laws and sent to prison. Then he was banished to Huang Zhou. He was a county magistrate of Mi Zhou, Xu Zhou, Hu Zhou, Hang Zhou, Ying Zhou and Yang Zhou early or late. At the beginning of Shao Sheng, because he involved in Yuan You Party he was banished to Hui Zhou county. When Hui Zong ascended the throne, he was remitted. He soon died in Chang Zhou. He is the greatest writer in the Northern Song and known to have brilliant contribution in poem, essay and ci-poetry. His ci-poem had a bold and unconstrained style. His " Dong Po Yue Fu " was handed down. Three hundred pieces of his ci-poem are still remained.

# Jiāng Chéng Zǐ
# 江　城　子

Sū Shì
蘇軾

Shí nián shēng sǐ liǎng máng māng
十 年 生 死 兩 茫 茫，

bù sī liāng, zì nán wāng
不 思 量 自 難 忘。

Qiān lǐ gū fén　wú chù huà qī liāng
千 里 孤 墳，無 處 話 淒 涼。

Zōng shǐ xiāng féng yīng bù shí
縱 使 相 逢 應 不 識，

chén mǎn miàn, bìn rú shuāng
塵 滿 面 鬢 如 霜。

Yè lái yōu mèng hú huán xiāng
夜 來 幽 夢 忽 還 鄉，

xiǎo xuān chuāng, zhèng shū zhuāng
小 軒 窗 正 梳 妝。

Xiāng gù wú yán, wéi yǒu lèi qiān hāng
相 顧 無 言 惟 有 淚 千 行。

Liào dé nián nián cháng duàn chù
料 得 年 年 腸 斷 處，

míng yuè yè, duǎn sōng gāng
明 月 夜 短 松 岡。

# Song of Riverside City

by Su Shi


For ten years the living and the dead,
Both have been in the dark,
I don't try to turn over it in my heart,
But forgetting is hard.
Your solitary grave is a thousand miles away,
No where to tell the dreary.
Even if we could meet,
I would not be recognitory,
My face is all covered with dust,
And temples as frost.

In a dim dream suddenly I returned at night.
At the chamber window,
You were dressing and making up.
We looked at each other without word,
Only a thousand lines of tears poured.
Year after year, as expected,
You must be heartbroken at the place,
Where the moon is bright at night,
And the ridge is short,
With small pines covered.

# Appreciation

In 1075, Su Shi was an official administering Mi Zhou (now Zhu county in Shandong Province). This ci poem was written in January that year to mourn for his wife, Wang Fu. When Wang was sixteen, she married Su Shi, She was a bright and virtuous woman and had knowledge and experience. There was deep love between them. Unfortunately she died in 1065 when she was only 27. Next year she was buried in Sichuan (Province), their hometown. After ten years' drifting along in official circles, Su Shi expressed his deep feelings for his deceased wife.

This poem made a start from their ten years separation, came straight to the point: the living and the dead parted for ever. " Both have been in the dark " means he and his wife missed each other for ten years but they hadn't heard anything from each other. The word " both " means two sides, " in the dark " means the bleak situation they had, but in reality he was writing his own measureless melancholy. The first sentence narrats both the fact and emotions, deciding on a basic tune of mourning the death of his wife through the whole sheet. Such an opening has not seen before.

Though the author often thought of his deceased wife, he said conversely: " I don't try to turn over it ", then he wrote again the other way round: " forgetting is hard ". Such cadenced description showed his wife's image came back to his mind constantly and his love was very deep. If we say the first three sentences describe the long time the living and the dead being apart, the following sentences write the far distance they were scattered. At that time the author was in Mi Zhou which was in Shandong Province, his deceased wife was buried in Sichuan. So he said: " Your solitary grave is a thousand miles away ". She alone buried there, so far away and so lonely, she must have her bosom filled with wretched feelings, but she was all by herself. " Nowhere to tell the dreary ". Complaining tearfully his wife's miserable was just like complaining his own. Not only because they stayed at two places far apart but also because they were in two different world which couldn't be surpassed. There were far move miserable than these. In these ten years, since his political view did not conform to the political reform, he was reduced to a lower rank several times. His political career failed. He was in a very difficult position. So his appearance withered too early. He said: " Even if we could meet, I would not be recognitory. My face is all covered with dust and temples as frost. "

The first part narrates the fact expressing the writer's deep love for his wife. The second part describes the dream. A word " suddenly " brings the readers to a dream blurred and dim. The writer dreams that he is back at night. He Said: " At the chamber window, you were dressing and making up. " This sentence tells us that in the dream he saw his wife the same as usual. She made up herself before the window. Here the life of man and wife in their youth was reappeared. Once he and his wife meet again after a long separation, they must have a lot to say, but the train of thought is confusing. " We looked at each other without word, only a thousand lines of tears poured ". This sentence is a feature, no sound but with tears, which has greater artistic effect than any other words. The above all mentioned dream. The last three sentences narrates sigh with emotion after awakening. It said: " As expected, year after year, you must be heartbroken at the place, where the moon is bright at night, and the ridge is short, with small pine covered. " The writer imagine that in the remote wilderness thousand miles away when the moonlight night came, on the short ridge, which covered with small pine, his wife must be heartbroken year after year in thinking of him. The writer describes his wife's state of mind, in fact, he was describing himself. He mourned for his wife endlessly. He paints the scenery only to express his feelings. The music lingers in the air.

Using ci-poem mourns for the dead, which was initiated by Su Shi. Thus it could be seen that Su Shi's developing spirit in enlarging ci-poem realm was great. This ci-poem's language is easy to understand. The love for his wife is sincerely. Readers can not but be touched deeply.

# Dié Liàn huā
# 蝶 戀 花

Sū Shì
蘇 軾


Huā tuì cán hóng qīng xìng xiǎo
花 褪 殘 紅 青 杏 小 ，

yàn zǐ fēi shí, lǜ shuǐ rén jiā rǎo
燕 子 飛 時 綠 水 人 家 繞 。

Zhī shàng liǔ mián chuī yòu shǎo
枝 上 柳 綿 吹 又 少 ，

tiān yá hé chù wú fāng cǎo
天 涯 何 處 無 芳 草 ！


Qiáng lǐ qiū qiān qiáng wài dào
牆 裏 鞦 韆 牆 外 道 ，

qiáng wài xíng rén
牆 外 行 人 ，

qiáng lǐ jiā rén xiào
牆 裏 佳 人 笑 。

Xiào jiàn bù wén shēng jiàn qiāo
笑 漸 不 聞 聲 漸 悄 ，

duō qíng què bèi wú qíng nǎo
多 情 卻 被 無 情 惱 。

# Butterflies Love Flowers

by Su Shi


Flowers have taken off their last blossom,
But green apricots are still small.
Swallows are flying.
Around the green water and wall.
On the branches willow floss blown being fewer,
At the and of the world,
what place is without fragrant grass?

Inside the wall is a swing,
Outside it a path.
The pedestrian outside hear the beauty chuckling
Inside the wall.
Little by little,
The chuckling can't be heard,
and the sound quiet. Instead,
By the heartless,
The full affectionate is annoyed.

# Appreciation

This is a ci-poem signing over a subject, that is: Spring passses quickly and the beautiful woman is hard to find. In the first part the poet is sick at heart for the loss of spring. He says: " The flowers have lost their blossom. The green apricots are still small ". Purple swallows are flying lightly around the green water and wall. Willow floss are fluttering, fragrant grasses are boundless. These are the scenery of late spring and early summer. The poet describes these in order to express his sigh with emotion.

The second part describes the unrequited love of the pedestrian outside the wall. Inside the wall there was a beauty swinging and chuckling loudly. The pedestrian outside was enchanted and produced adoring thought. But the beauty inside was not aware of the pedestrian's existing. After the swinging, she left trippingly. Little by littel, the chuckling couldn't be heard. The pedestrian was annoyed.

The author was good at describing the characteristic scene of late spring and early summer and also knew how to express his emotion through describing scenery. " Last blossom " indicated the falling of the red flowers. There were not much left. " Take off " means the flowers' colour faded. The feelings were a step further. " Green apricots are still small " states clearly that summer has just come. Through writing the scenery the first sentence tells the season. The second and third sentences explain place. There was a family on the scene. In the air the swallows were flying. Around the house the green water was flowing. Describing the family is laying a hint to foreshadow later developments. On the next part, " the beauty chuckling inside the wall " . That was the very house. The word " around " describes the swallow around the water, the green water around the wall, the pedestrian around the house. Though one word, it makes you associate three things and truly reflected the actual scenery, very vividly. " On the branches willow floss blown being fewer " indicates the spring's returning. " What place is without fragrant grass " . If fragrant grasses are everywhere, they are growing luxuriantly, hundreds of flowers must have withered. Here the writer grieves at the passing of the spring again. Though he was exceedingly sentimental, the descriptions did not repeat.

The second part was especially wonderful. The whole part only had four sentences. The word " inside " and " outside " have been repeated several times. But we do not feel the repetition. The repeating itself in cycles gave you infinite interest instead. The young man thought himself full of affection, was reluctant to leave. The young woman was not even aware of his existance. She had gone away with her chuckling. This was a common sight in life, was not at all surprising. When the writer had a high degree of focus to describe this, to compare the pedestrian outside the wall with the beauty inside, his full affection with the heartless, the chuckling with the annoyed clevery, which obtains a philosophy summary that " the full affectionate is annoyed by the heartless ", the lines have become a remarkable piece of writing, which produced very high artistic effect.

As one first reads this poem, he may feel that the comedy of the unrequited love in the second part doesn't seem to be in tune with the mood of the grief at the passing spring in the first part. Perhaps this is because he does not make a correct appraisal of the internal relations between these two parts. In fact, the first part describes " when the flowers fall into the flowing water, the spring has gone. " which set off " the beauty is hard to find " in the second part. So both parts all sigh over the fact that " good time doesn't last long ", and " flourishing days pass quickly ". They were accomplished without any interruption. Su Shi was loyal to the court. He was a most faithful official. But he was banished to an outlying place. This ci-poem expresses his state of mind when he was transfered to Hui Zhou. Couldn't we say he was " the full affectionate who was annoyed by the heartless " ? At that time he was in an adverse circumstances, as the willow floss destroyed by wind and rain. Wasn't " On the branches the willow floss blown being fewer " also a line describing his own circumstances?

# Què Qiáo Xiān
## 鵲 橋 仙

### Qín Guān
#### 秦 觀

Xiān yún nòng qiǎo
纖 雲 弄 巧，

fēi xīng chuán hèn
飛 星 傳 恨，

yín hàn tiáo tiáo àn dù
銀 漢 迢 迢 暗 度。

Jīn fēng yù lù yī xiāng féng
金 風 玉 露 一 相 逢，

biàn shèng quē rén jiān wú shù
便 勝 卻 人 間 無 數。

Róu qíng shì shuǐ
柔 情 似 水，

jiā qī rú mèng
佳 期 如 夢，

rěn gù què qiáo guī lù
忍 顧 鵲 橋 歸 路。

Liǎng qíng ruò shì jiǔ cháng shí
兩 情 若 是 久 長 時，

yòu qǐ zài zhāo zhāo mù mù
又 豈 在 朝 朝 暮 暮。

# Immortal at the Magpie Bridge

by Qin Guan

Fine clouds float and change,
Hunreds of clever shapes emerging.
The flying stars transmit regret,
Milky Way far away was secretly passed.
During the time of jade dew and golden wind,
Once they meet,
Far better than man's world, theirs must.

Tender feelings as water,
Nuptial day as dream,
Who will be hardhearted enough,
To see her magpie bridge way home?
If two hearts are permanent,
How could they care about,
Being together from morning till night.

# Appreciation

This ci-poem adoptes the legend that " the Cowherd and the Girl Weaver meet in Heaven in the seventh evening of the seventh moon ". The common people say: " The Cowherd and the weaver Maid get together on each seventh of July. In that evening the magpies will build a bridge by their own bodies for the poor couple to pass across the Milky Way. In man's world, people display fruits and melons in the courtyard to beg for cunning. " Though the writer described the scene in Heaven, he really wrote what he had seen and thought when he looked up at the stars on the seventh eve of July.

The first three sentences of the first part describes autumn clouds, thin and slight. " The fine clouds float and change, emerging hundreds of clever shapes. " tells us that the clouds drift from place to place, which are changeable and make one associate them with the nimble hands of Weaving Maid. " Flying stars transmit regret " says that the Cowherd star and Weaver Maid star glimmer unceasingly, which seemed to contain endless disconsolate regret. Perhaps they hated to be separated in different places and hard to meet with each other. Only on the eve of the seventh of July could they pour out their hearts. " Milky Way far away is secretly passed ". Milky Way namely is the Galaxy. This sentence describes: The curtain of night was falling. The star's light were faint. Their gloomy mood was numerous. However, they had passed the Milky Way. In the fourth sentence " golden wind and jade dew " shows the season. The Cowherd and Weaver Maid meet at the time when autumn wind blows valiantly and white dew first falls. " Once they meet, theirs must be far better than man's world ". The meaning of this sentence is their love is very deep. Once they meet, their meeting is far better than the countless meetings in man's world, because their feelings are true and loves are earnest, which are far more noble and valuable than the vulgar emotion and interest in the world.

In the first three sentences of the second part, the poet spread his

150

strong imagination towards the sky. He imagined that the two stars met in the magpies' bridge. Their affections for each other must have been very deep. They must have recounted their inner feelings. Though they were separated by the Milky Way, their hearts were long drawn-out. But the naptial day of the seventh eve would pass in the twinkling of an eye. As a dream their happy reunion would soon become parting. Who would hardhearted enough to see the magpies flying away, the way back broken? After saying goodbye in a hurry, he would see her off lonely, gazing at her receding figure disappear at a distance. But the last two sentences came out of conventional patterns and had a new approach. That is, whether the two hearts are permanent, they do not depend on being together from morning till night. This sentence went a step further again to describe their deep love. These lines become a much-told tale through the ages.

## A Brief Account of the Author's Life

Qin Guan(1049-1100) styled himself Tai Xu, later changed it into Shao You. Scholars call him Mr Huai Hai. He is a native of Jiangsu Province, Gao You County. In 1085 he became a successful candidate in the highest imperial examinations. At the beginning years of Zhe Zong, Yuan You, he was recommended into the capital to be an official early or late. He and Huan Ting Jian, Chao Bu Zhi, Zhang Lei were appreciated and promoted by Su Shi. They discussed writings and judged poems. They learnt from each other by knowledge. They were celebrated for " Four Scholars of Su Family ". At the beginning years of Shao Shen, he was banished to the Southern part of the country, because he had associated with Su Shi. In 1100, he was called back but died when he returned by way of Teng Zhou(now Teng county of Guangxi Province). His works had " Huai Hai Lay Buddhist Shorter or Longer Lines ". The total is in 46 volumes.

# Rú Mèng Lìng
# 如　夢　令

**Lǐ Qīng-zhào**
李　清　照

Cháng jì xī tíng rì mù
常　記　溪　亭　日　暮，

chén zuì bù zhī guī lù
沉　醉　不　知　歸　路。

Xìng jìn wǎn húi zhōu
興　盡　晚　回　舟，

wù rù ǒu huā shēn chù
誤　入　藕　花　深　處。

Zhēng dù　zhēng dù
爭　渡，爭　渡，

jīng qǐ yī tān ōu lù
驚　起　一　灘　鷗　鷺。

# As in a Dream: Song

by Li Qing-zhao


I remembered the stream arbor at sunset,
Getting drunk we didn't know the way back.
After thoroughly enjoying ourselves,
We headed home late by boat,
Going astray into the depth of lotus blossoms.
Struggling to push through,
Struggling to push through,
Startling the herons in the sandy beach.

# Appreciation

Li Qing-zhao's "As In A Dream: Song" is a bright pearl in the earlier stage of her ci-poems. It manifests a woman ci-poet's figure, lively, forthright, sincere and having a deep love for life, and her deep beautiful inner world and high elegant joy of life.

The first sentence say that the author remembered once she had been to an arbor by a stream. It was sunset, there were several people in her touring party. Because they had drunk a great deal they were tipsy and did not know the way home. They were keenly interest in going sight-seeing. They were merry and lively, indulging in pleasure and forgetting everything. The ci-poem reflected the temperament and interest of literati and officialdom and revealed the author's bold, uninhibited, free and easy character. The author and the others set out cheerfully and returned after thoroughly enjoying themselves.

They headed back late by boat. It was hard to avoid going astray into depths of lotus blossoms. The ci-poem was very witty. It describes that the tourists' tipsy feeling did not abate, not did their interest in going on an excursion decrease, they did not care about the trouble to go wrong. So they must struggle to pass through. When we read these words, we seem to hear the oars beating the water, see the boat going forward vigorously and see the tourists carefree, talking and laughing. Because of the speed crossing the stream the herons were startled in the sandy beach. The reiterative sentences "Struggling ··· through" vividly expresses the tourists' mood for enjoyment. It was just because they struggled to push through, the herons sleeping there, startled by the noise, flapped their wings and flew away. The herons serve as a contrast to make the heroine's figure more natural, unrestrained and innocent.

This ci-poem vividly depicts a natural scene. The language is simple and fine which characterizes the early works of Li Qing-zhao. She wrote her new thoughts in simple, straightforward words.

154

# A Brief Account of the Author's Life

Li Qing-zhao (1084-1156) styled herself Yi An Lay Buddhist. She is a native of Li Cheng (now Shang Dong Province Jinan County). She married Zhao Ming-chen, an epigrapher. She could write essays, rhythmical prose, shi-poems and ci-poems. She could also paint pictures and research epigraphy. Before the Jing Kang incident, she lived in Li Cheng, Bian Jing、 Qing Zhou、 Lai Zhou. After the incident, her husband died. She escaped South and wandered in Jiangsu, Zhejiang, Anhui, Jiangxi and so on. Her works have been incorporated into " A Collection of Li Yi-an ", " Shu Yu Ci-poems " and " Yi An Lay Buddhist Collected Works ". But all have been lost. Her style of writings is delicate and pretty, Which exerted a tremendous influence on the literary world of the Southern Song. Poets such as Xing Jia-xuan, Lu You and others benifitted considerably.

# Rú Mèng Lìng
# 如 夢 令

Lǐ Qīng-zhào
李 清 照

Zuó yè yǔ shū fēng zhòu
昨 夜 雨 疏 風 驟，

nóng shuì bù xiāo cán jiǔ
濃 睡 不 消 殘 酒。

Shì wèn juǎn lián rén
試 問 捲 簾 人，

què dào hǎi táng yī jiù
卻 道 海 棠 依 舊。

Zhī fǒu  Zhī fǒu
知 否？知 否？

Yīng shì lǜ féi hóng shòu
應 是 綠 肥 紅 瘦。

# As in a Dream: Song

by Li Qing-zhao

Last night,
The rain scattered light,
But the wind blew swift,
Deeply sleeping did not dispel,
The wine effects.
Trying to ask the maid,
Rolling up the screen,
But she answered:
" The crab-apple blossoms look just the same. "
" Haven't you seen? Haven't you seen?
It should be found that,
The fat is green,
But the red is thin. "

# Appreciation

This ci-poem writes ci-poet's sensitive to the change of the nature and her concern about the fine things. Let's see how she described the scenery. " The rain scattered light, but the wind blew swift ", that is, the rain was small but the wind blew hard. How did she describe the man? " Deeply sleeping did not dispel the wine effect. " " Deeply sleeping " means sleeping soundly " Did not dispel the wine effect " means did not sleep off the wine, then how to write the flowers. " The fat is green but the red is thin. " Green replaces the leaves, while red, the flowers. In late spring, the leaves are growing luxuriantly, but the flowers are falling. Such a careful depiction, gives readers a very bright and striking impression, especially the sentences " The fat is green but the red is thin ", which are very pure and fresh, and in gaudy colour. The images are really true to life. Those words have never been said by anyone else. The rhyme scheme is also excellent, such as: zhòu, jiě, jiù, fǒu and shòu, are all alternate with falling and rising tone, pleasant to the ear. Then let's see the question and answer. " Trying to ask the maid rolling up the screen " led to the conversation between the heroine and the maid. " But she answered: ' The crab-apple blossoms look just the same.' " Here the writer only wrote the answer, the question of the heroine was omitted. Because from the answer we could see what the question was. Obviously the question and the answer did not suit each other. The question was full of affection concerning after a night's rain and wind how the crab-apple is, but the answer is very indifferent. Because the maid is careless, which forces the heroine to ask another sentimental question " Haven't you seen? Haven't you seen? " And she pointed out: " It should be found that the green is fat, but the red is thin. " The heroine, out of concern for flowers, asked the question seriously. In order to value every flowers she refuted the maid sincerely. The concluding sentence: " It should be found that the fat is green, but the red is thin ", contained boundless sad and implicit the poet's mood, sorry for " good flowers do not often blossom " .

This is only a small ci-poem. Just in a few words the poet tells us so much feelings, the rhymes are so beautiful too. All these show that the poet's creative power is excellent.

# Wǔ Líng Chūn
# 武 陵 春

Lǐ Qīng-zhào
李 清 照

Fēng zhù chén xiāng huā yǐ jìn
風 住 塵 香 花 已 盡，

rì wǎn juàn shū tōu
日 晚 倦 梳 頭。

Wù shì rén fēi shì shì xiū
物 是 人 非 事 事 休，

yù yǔ lèi xiān liū
欲 語 淚 先 流。

Wén shuō shuāng Xī chūn shàng hǎo
聞 說 雙 溪 春 尚 好，

yě nǐ fàn qīng zhōu
也 擬 泛 輕 舟。

Zhǐ kǒng shuāng xī zé měng zhōu
只 恐 雙 溪 舴 艋 舟，

zài bù dòng xǔ duō chōu
載 不 動 許 多 愁。

# Spring in Peach-blossom Land

by Li Qing-zhao

Wind has stopped,
Dust is fragrant,
All the flowers have fallen.
It's late in the morning,
But I get tired of combing.
Things remain,
He passed away,
All is nothing.
I tried to speak but tears falling.

I have heard that at Twin Brook,
The spring is still fair
I intended to float in a locust boat too.
Only I fear that the tiny vehicle there
Can't load with grief a great deal.

# Appreciation

In September of 1134, Jinren(Nuzhen nationality in North China) dispatched troops advancing south. Seeking asylum, Qing-zhao set out from Linan(now Hangzhou)to Jinghua. This ci-poem was written in the spring of 1135 when she was 52.

The first sentence in the first part says: the flowers in full bloom were hit by fierce wind. When it stopped, the flowers were all faded and fallen into the dust. so the dust was fragrant. This sentence also describes her own wandering life. Jinren's intruding over, her life was destroyed. The second sentence says: " It's late in the morning, I get tired of combing. " She was disheartened. So the sun was already up, she still did not comb her hair. The third sentence says: " Things remain, but he passed away ". Therein lay the crux of the problem. Her husband died and her life changed greatly. She thought: " All is nothing, I tried to speak but tears flowing. " Read this sentence who would not sympathize with her?

In the first three sentences of the second part, " still fair ", " intend to float " and " only fear " depicts her inner world very well. We all know that Qing-zhao loved to go boating very much. When she was young, she wrote such lines: " After thoroughly enjoying ourselves, we headed home late by boat, going astray into the depth of the lotus blossoms. " How she wanted to shake off many old sores. Twin brook was a scenic spot of Jinghua. Of course, she intended to float in a locust boat. But why she did not go? She worried about her own grief which was too heavy to load by the little boat. The reason why she did not go told us how deep her grief was. Her description of the boat depicting her grief vividly.

Li Yu in his ci-poem said: " If (I am) asked, how much distress is in the heart? Just like a full river of spring water flowing east. " He draw a parallel between grief and water. The meaning implied is that the grief was as much as water. Li Qing-zhao gave grief weight and loaded it in a boat. She brought forth another new idea in the arts.

162

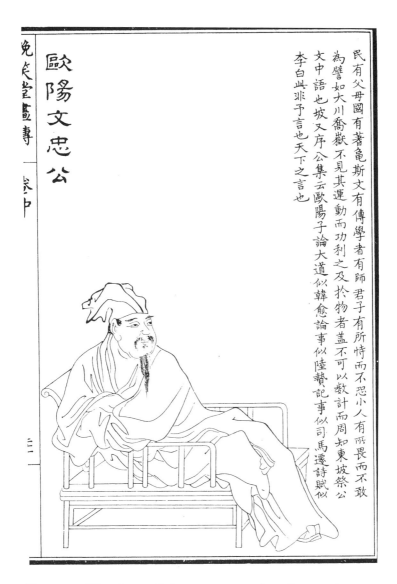

民有父母國有著龜斯文有傳學者有師　君子有所恃而不恐小人有所畏而不敢

為譬如大川喬嶽不見其運動而功利之及於物者蓋不可以數計而周知東坡祭公

文中語也坡又序公集云歐陽子論大道似韓愈論事似司馬遷詩賦似

李白此非予言也天下之言也

歐陽文忠公

Ou-yang Xiu: One of the representative figures in the
golden age of ci-poetry, Northern Song

# Pú Sà Mán
# 菩薩蠻

Lǐ Mí-xùn
李彌遜

Jiāng chéng fēng huǒ lián sān yuè
江 城 烽 火 連 三 月，

bù kān duì jiǔ cháng tíng bié
不 堪 對 酒 長 亭 別。

Xiū zuò duàn cháng shēng
休 作 斷 腸 聲，

lǎo lái wú lèi qīng
老 來 無 淚 傾。

Fēng gāo fān yǐng jí
風 高 帆 影 疾，

mù sòng zhōu hén bì
目 送 舟 痕 碧。

Jǐn zì jǐ shí lái
錦 字 幾 時 來？

Xūn fēng wú yàn huí
薰 風 無 雁 回。

# Deva-like Barbarian

by Li Mi-xun

In Jiang City flames of battle has three months running,
I can't bear facing,
The wine, to say good-bye on the long pavilion.
Don't make heartbroken sound,
So old as I have no tear pouring.

The Wind blows high,
The shadow of the sails speed wide.
I watch the boat trace blue.
When will the brocade words come true?
As the wind is fumigated,
No wild goose will tour.

# Appreciation

In the early years of the Southern Song Dynasty, Jin's troops advanced south on a large scale, which was pressing on towards Yongtze River. The situation was very critical. In order to keep away the chaos of war, the poet saw his wife off and wrote this poem.

The first sentence of the first part adopts Du Fu's line " Flames of battle has three months running ". The poet quoted this line to describe the war in Jiang city and pointed out the special environment of parting. Du Fu in those days found himself encircled by the rebel army of An Shi suddenly. He wanted to return but couldn't. In this ci-poem the couple lived together originally. Now the husband saw his wife off, the wife left her husband, they were compelled to be separated by the situation. So the author said: " I can't bear facing the wine to say good-bye on the long pavilion. " The following sentences: " Don't make heartbroken sound. So old as I have no tear pouring. " started from dynamic expression during parting and then draw a wretched parting picture. The sad words the author used to console his wife set off his wife's mood, who shed bitter tears at that very moment, and also expressed the poet's extremely sad inner world. At such a time when the old couple had to separate, the poet claimed to " have no tear pouring ". Whether he had experienced the hardship of life, his mind was filled with grief, his tears have been decocted dry, or he controlled his feelings with matchless stamina and did not allow his tears to pour in order to console his wife, no one knew. Perhaps he had both.

The second part describes a sorrowful parting scene. " The wind blows high. The shadows of the sails speed wide. I watch the boat trace blue. " The wife left by boat. The husband was in a disturbed state of mind. He gazed the boat passing without saying a word. In this static picture, clearly there must be the poet's feelings surging which contained many sad words tearing the bottom of his heart. The husband was kept in suspense about his wife's leaving alone. The wife also worried about her husband being left in turmoil and chaos of war. Standing on the stem, the wife overwhelmed by grief, the husband on shore raised his head and looked front, driven to distraction. This was the picture the second part given to us. " The wind blows high " truly unfolded the sails relying on the wind leaving quickly and the poet's complex spirit under such circumstances. In fact, the wind did not likely blow high, the shadows of the sail was not likely fast either, merely because the poet did not resign himself to see his wife's boat disappear too soon, he could only watch the boat trace blue, without a word. Those sentences just show his regret at parting. The last two sentences say: " When will the brocade words come true? No wild goose will tour as the wind is fumigated. " " Fumigated wind " is the south wind. The meaning of these sentences are when summer came, the south wind began to blow, the wild goose flew north. Though his wife wrote letters, no bird would bring the letter for her. These two sentences showed that their future couldn't be foreseen. Now they parted, whether they could meet again, it was hard to predict.

The poet used simple, straight forward style of writing to describe the whole course of seeing his wife off, which wrote down the tragic atmosphere and his true feelings, not at all hiding, so it was stirring and made the readers shed tears.

## A Brief Account of the Author's Life

Li Mi-xun (1089-1153) styled himself Shi Zhi. Jun Xi Weng is his assumed name. He is a native of Lian Jiang (now belongs to FuJian Province). He lived in Wu county (now belongs to Jiangsu Province). He was a successful candidate in the highest imperial examinations in 1109. He stood for resisting Jin and fought against negotiating peace with them. He was excluded by Qin Kuai. He lived in seclusion in his later years. His works was collected in " A Collection of Jun Xi ".

# Jiǎn Zì Mù Lán Hūa
# 減字木蘭花

Zhū Shū-zhèn

朱　淑　眞


Dú xīng dú zuò

獨　行　獨　坐，

dú chàng dú chóu hái dú wò

獨　唱　獨　酬　還　獨　臥。

Zhù lì shāng shén

佇立　傷　神，

wú nài chūn hán zhū mō rén

無奈　春　寒　著　摸　人。


Cǐ qíng shuí jiàn

此　情　誰　見？

Lèi xǐ cán zhuāng wú yī bàn

淚洗　殘　妝　無一　半。

Chóu bìng xiāng rěng

愁　病　相　仍，

tī jìn hán dēng mèng bù chéng

剔　盡　寒　燈　夢不　成。

168

# Magnolia Being Reduced in Words

by Zhu Shu-zhen

Pace alone sit alone,
Compose alone reply alone and still lie alone.
Standing still for long,
I am grief stricken.
Having no choice,
I can only be teased at spring cold discretion.

Who knows this feelings?
Tears washed the remnant makeup,
That left not a half.
Sadness and illness come one after another.
All the cold lampwick being rejected,
Dreams do not come up.

# Appreciation

Zhu Shu-zhen was a famous woman ci-poet in the Song Dynasty. When she was young, she had a good love affair, but her parents broke up them, and forced her to marry to a vulgar official. They did not have similar tastes and interests. Later, she had to leave her husband and returned to her mother's home, lived there alone, disheartened and dejected all her life.

This ci-poem reflects her adversity. It had a very strange style. At the very beginning it says the writer neither felt like to pace nor to sit; composing, replying and talking to herself were completely not right. She was terribly upset. She was unable to cope with herself. It was like a complete flames raging fiercely in her heart. The heart was overwhelmed by grief. After agitated for a while she calmed down. She stood there with fixed attention overtaxed her nerves alone. She tormented herself with such a mood that she was not aware of the time past quickly. She only felt the spring cold assailing her.

Continually she said: " Who knows this feelings? " This words expresses her solitary feelings with emphasis. Then she added: " Sadness and illness come one after another " , she could only face the cold lamp weeping. So " Tears washed the remnant make-up that left not a half " . Her grief was without end. Though " All the cold lampwick were rejected " , she could not sleep.

This ci-poem was written in a pungent style. It describes a woman who was deeply grieved, solitary and sleepless at night. Her every act and every moving sight were really described truly to life.

The first two sentences write from pacing, sitting to a poem's composing and replying to express her solitary life. There are only eleven words, five " alone " s were used, and using these words to form five phrases. In syllables they were special too. So these lines could deeply reflect the author's miserable encounter. The whole poem is compact and well organized. It stresses the subject and gives a vivid description to a woman who was sad and ill. Hence it is worthy to esteem.

## A Brief Account of the Author's Life

Zhu Shu-zhen, styled herself You Xi Lay Buddhist. She is a native of Zhejiang, Qian Tang (now Hangzhou). When she was born and died, nobody knows. From the contents of her ci-poem, she might live in the end of the Northern Song Dynasty and the early of the Southern Song Dynasty. She was from an official's family. As a child, she was well versed in painting and poetry. She was a famous woman writer in the Song Dynasty. When she was young she had a bright and clear disposition. She had a fine love affair, but her parents broke up them and forced her to marry to a vulgar official. She did not have a happy marriage, died of illness. Her works has been collected in "A Collection of Heartbroken".

# Sù Zhōng Qíng
# 訴 衷 情*

Lù Yóu
陸 游


Dāng nián wàn lǐ mì fēng hóu
當 年 萬 里 覓 封 侯，

pī mǎ shù liáng zhōu
匹 馬 戍 梁 州。

Guān hé mèng duàn hé chù
關 河 夢 斷 何 處？

Chēn àn jìn dīa qíu
塵 暗 舊 貂 裘。


Hú wèi miè
胡 未 滅，

bīn xiān qīu
鬢 先 秋，

lèi kōng liú
淚 空 流。

Cǐ shēng shuí liào
此 生 誰 料，

xīn zài tiān shān
心 在 天 山，

shēn lǎo cāng zhōu
身 老 滄 洲。

# Telling of Innermost Feelings

by Lu You

In those years I travelled ten thousand li,
To hunt for being granted marquis.
I guarded Liangzhou single-handed, frontier.
Where are my dreams,
Of guarding the passes and rivers broken?
Only dust has darkened,
My old coat marten.

The tartars have not been wiped out.
My temple hair had turned grey around.
Tears have fallen in vain.
Who would have expected that this life,
My heart should be on the Tain Mountains,
While my body grows old in Cang Zhou.

---

* The Ci-poem Rules of Wan Shu said: People of Song Dynasty all used this style.

# Appreciation

When Lu You was two years old, his country, the Northern Song was destroyed by the Jin Dynasty. So during the youth and the prime of his life, he always cherished the ideal of the expedition to the north of China and the recovery of the lost territory. When he was 48, he reached South Zhen, the north west front (now Shanxi Province, Hanzhong county) and had a hand in military operations. It was a pity that in the court of the Southern Song the capitulationist clique sought momentary ease, his ideal and desire could not be realized. He had only his bosom filled with grief and indignation. Such feelings were often shown in his poems. This ci-poem was one of the famous pieces in his later years.

In the first two sentences of the first part the author looked back from now, all sorts of feelings welled up in his mind. " I guarded Liangzhou frontier, singlehanded. " was directed the life when he joined the army in South Zhen. " I travelled ten thousand li to hunt for being granted marquis " quoted Ban Cao's story secretly. Ban was a general of Han Dynasty, resisting aggression of Xiongnu and making contributions time and again. These two sentences write out his high spirit of those years. He thought he could do a deed of merit for his country, but he did not. His ideal was only a dream. So he said " Where are my dream of guarding the passes and rivers broken? " It did not only become a dream, but accomplished nothing as well. The sentence: " Only dust has darkened my old marten coat. " describes that he was down and out. The poet here quoted the story of Su Qin. Su was the prime minister of six countries in the Warring States (475-221 B.C.) He stood for allying six countries to resist Qin Dynasty. At first no king believed him, so he was in dire straits.

The first three sentences of the second part: " The tartars have not been wiped out. My temple hair had turned grey around. Tears have flown in vain. " were parallelized sentences. Integrated " The tartars have not been wiped out ", with " I travelled ten thousand li, to hunt for being granted marquis. " of the first part, we would see: in order to wipe out enemies he travelled ten thousand li. But the enemies were not wiped out, he himself had been old. " My temple hair had turned grey. " was his lament. Originally, he should join the army in his robust years, imbued with a spirit that can conquer tartars. Now the tartars were the same, he himself grew old. So " tears have flown " . It was of no avail. The concluding remarks say: " Who would have expected that this life, My heart should be on the Tian Mountains, While my body grows old in Cang Zhou. " Those words are very heavy. " My heart should be on the Tian Mountains " was quoted from the classical allusions that Xue Ren Gui's three arrows achieved the stability of Tian Mountain (Xue was a history hero, Xue Ren Gui went on an expedition to the east. ) The focal point was connecting this line with " ten thousand li " and " Liangzhou " . " Tian Mountain " is in the North West of China. Dispatching troops to North West and putting down the rebellion in the Central Plains were ideals the author bore in mind constantly. But now he was old. Before the national affairs he was powerless. He could not solve the contradiction of " My heart should be on the Tian Mountains, while my body grows old in Cang Zhou " (a place for ancients to withdraw from society). He wished to do a deed of merit subjectively, but objectively he was senile and could do nothing. " Who would have expected that this life " he was so contradictory. Who would live in such a contradiction? These conclusion told the readers that this was the crime of the humiliation and capitulation policy of the court. Not saying straightly but using a question could call for deeper thought.

The structure of this ci-poem is different from the others. Generally, the first part and the second part each occupies a half. If the first part describes past, the second part should describe the present. In this poem two sentences of the first part describe past, the other two, present. In the second part every sentence describes present but is connected with the past. We can't devide them into two. In choice of words, the poet used strong contrast to express his intense mood. What's more, he used a great many literary quotations, such as: "ten thousand li to hunt for being granted marquis", "dust has darkened my old marten coat", "on the Tian Mountain" and "in Cang Zhou". If you did not know that the poet was using literary quotations, you can still understand the ci-poem. If you knew them, you would feel more cordial. This is the language of this ci poem that is worth pondering.

## A Brief Account of the Author's Life

Lu You (1125-1210) styled himself Wu Guan, assumed name Fang Weng. He is a native of Shan Yin (now Shao Xin county Zhejiang Province). In the year of Shao Xin 32nd, he was granted Jin Shi and then was a government official all his life. He was made a Wei Nan Count in his later years. He died at the age of 85. He lived when the two countries, Song and Jin, stood facing each other in South and North. The sacred land of the Song Dynasty was split, wars were numerous, the court affairs of Song were dark, people suffered a lot. He cherished an ideal of the expedition of Central Plains and the recovery of the lost territory, using poems as an weapon to struggle for it. He is a famous patriotic poet of the Southern Song. It is a pity he could not realize his political aspiration. In the artistic creation of poem he carried on the good tradition of Qu Yuan, Tao Yuan Ming, Du Fu and Su Shi, and is a brilliant poet having profound influence in Chinese literature history. He wrote many books during his life time, such as: "Collected works of Wei Nan", "Jian Nan Poem Manuscripts", "Fang Weng Ci-poems", "South Tang Books" and "Old Xue An's Notes".

蘇文公

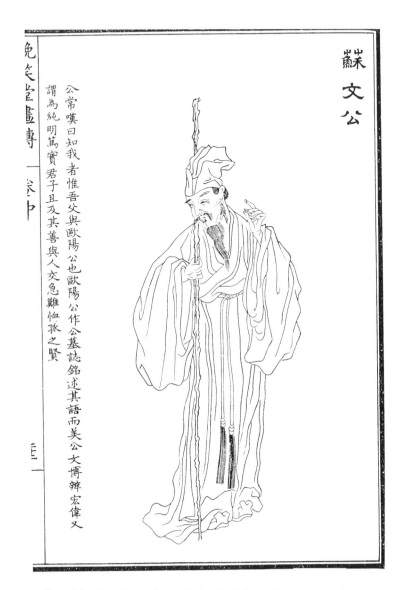

公常嘆曰知我者惟吾父與歐陽公也歐陽公作公墓誌銘述其語而美公文博辯宏偉又謂為純明篤實君子且及其善與人交急難恤孤之賢

Su shi: The founder of the bold and unconstrained
school of ci-poems

# Chǒu Nú Er Jìn
# 醜奴兒近 *

Xin Qì-jí
辛棄疾

Qiān fēng yún qǐ
千 峰 雲 起，

zhòu yǔ yī shà ér jià
驟 雨 一 霎 兒 價。

Gēng yuǎn shù xié yáng
更 遠 樹 斜 陽，

fēng jīng zěn shēng tú huà
風 景 怎 生 圖 畫？

Qīng qí mài jiǔ
青 旗 賣 酒，

shān nà pàn bié yǒu rén jiā
山 那 畔 別 有 人 家。

Zhǐ xiāo shān shuǐ guāng zhōng
只 消 山 水 光 中，

wú shì guò zhè yī xià
無 事 過 這 一 夏。

# Jin of Ugly Slaves

by Xin Qi-ji

Among thousand peaks black clouds roll,
In a moment, pelting down,
A heavy shower.
Then, a setting sun
Hanging on the distant plant,
So beautiful who can paint?
Under the blue flag,
A wineshop sells spirits.
On that side of the mountain,
There is another homestead.
I only need to live brilliantly,
In the mountain and river,
For nothing,
Passing this summer.

---

\* The register of this tune, according to the note of " The rules of Ci-poems of Wan Shu " book 4, was " Chou Nu Er Man ".

Wǔ zuī xǐng shí
午 醉 醒 時，

sōng chuāng zhú hù
松　窗　竹　戶，

wàn qiān xiāo sǎ
萬　千　瀟　灑。

Yě niǎo fēi lái
野　鳥　飛　來，

yòu shì yī bān xián xiá
又　是　一　般　閒　暇。

Quē guài bái ōu
卻　怪　白　鷗，

qù zhuó rén yù xià wèi xià
覷　着　人　欲　下　未　下。

Jiù méng dū zài
舊　盟　都　在，

xīn lái mò shì
新　來　莫　是，

bié yǒu shuō huà
別　有　說　話？

180

I drank before noon.
When I have come to,
Outside the door
There were the pine and bamboo,
Which was natural and unrestrained.
A wild bird came,
That's another kind of leisure.
Yet the white gull behaved quite strange,
He stole a glance at me,
As if longing to go down but afraid,
Old alliances are all here.
Can the new comer,
Has other idea?

# Appreciation

This is a ci-poem writing scenery. Bo Shan lies to the east of Yong Feng twenty li away (now Jiangxi Guang Feng). In ancient times, it was called Tong Yuan Feng, later changed into Bo Shan. When Xin Qi-ji lived in Shang Yao, he often travelled to and fro in the Bo Shan path. In this ci-poem he described Bo Shan in simple and straight forward style of writing.

In the first two sentences of the first part, the poet tells us: When he hurried on with his journey in Bo Shan path, between the peaks, black clouds blotted out the sky. The rain was pelting down. " In a moment " means the time was very short. In summer, the rain often come swiftly and violently, and go agilely too. So " in a moment " has double meanings. One is the rain coming suddenly, the other is it stops abruptly. The third sentence says: The setting sun was hanging on the tip of the trees far away. The scenery in Bo Shan path originally was very beautiful. Now after a shower, it was naturally very pure and fresh, bright and clear, delicate and charming. But the poet did not say how beautiful it was, but said " who can paint? " Of course, a painting was always the most beautiful thing in one's brain, here Xin Qi-ji went still a step further. He used a rhetorical question. The meaning is: the scenery here nobody could paint. That is to say the scenery was even more beautiful than painting. He esteemed the scenery to the summit. Then he used a close-up, pointed out that on that side of the mountain there were a wine shop hanging blue flag. The poet would have a deeper feeling to the green mountain when there was a wine shop selling spirits. " Sells spirits " were not words describing scenery but buried a hint foreshadowing later description. Because there was a wine shop sold spirits, the poet wanted " in the brilliant mountain and river " " passing this summer for nothing " .

The next part continues from the preceeding one. The poet says: he drank before noon and was a bit tipsy. Awakening from a sleep he looked around, all the scenery made him relaxed and happy. So he writes straightly the pine and bamboo outside the door, after the washing of the rain they became extremely quiet and beautiful. Besides a wild bird came, as if it would accompany the poet. The bird was leisurely and carefree, just like the poet. it's surprising that the old friend of the poet, the white gull looked at him secretly. As if it wanted to go down but was afraid. It is obvious that it had a misgiving about the poet. So the poet talks about it humorously. He says that we formed an alliance. The old treaty was still there. This time you came here. Did you have other idea to tell me? What is actually meant is that: " Did you forget your promise and did not want to be my friend? "

## A Brief Account of the Author's Life

Xin Qi-ji (1140-1207) styled himself You An, assumed name Jia-Xuan. He is a native of Jinan, Shandong. When he was a teenager, he lived in the North, which was occupied by Jin. He joined righteous army led by Geng Jin. He rushed into the enemy's campsite and captured betrayed general Zhang An-guo. After going to the South across Yangtze River, he submitted written statements to the emperor many times, advocated resisting Jin, recovering the Central Plains and unifying the country. But his proposition was not accepted. On the contrary, he met with exclusion and was attacked. He was relieved of his post and stayed at home idly in Jianxi countryside for 20 years. At the years of Kai Xi, the court proposed a Northern expedition, he once took up the post of county magistrate of Zhenjiang, but soon he was impeached and lost his job again. He was so worried and indignant, that he turned into disease and died. He is a famous patriotic poet. His ci-poem exerts a tremendous influence to later ages. He has written many poems and ci-poems, such as " Jia Xuan Shorter or Longer Lines ". Only 600 pieces of his ci-poems still remain.

# Qīng Píng Lè
# 清　平　樂

Xīn Qì-jì
辛棄疾

Máo yán dī xiǎo
茅　檐　低　小，

xī shàng qīng qīng cǎo
溪　上　青　青　草。

Zuì lǐ wú yīn xiāng mèi hǎo
醉　裏　吳　音　相　媚　好，

bái fǎ shuí jiā wēng ǎo
白　髮　誰　家　翁　媼？

Dà ér chú dòu xī dōng
大　兒　鋤　豆　溪　東，

zhōng ér zhèng zhí jī lóng
中　兒　正　織　鷄　籠。

Zuì xǐ xiǎo ér wú lài
最　喜　小　兒　無　賴，

xī tóu wò bō lián péng
溪　頭　臥　剝　蓮　蓬。

# Pure Serene Music

by Xin Qi-ji

Low and small are the thatched eaves.
Over the stream are green and green grasses.
Happily getting drunk,
We feel flattered by southern accents.
Who can they be
That elderly couple with hair whitening?

My eldest son is hoeing beans,
On the eastern bank of the stream.
The middle one is weaving,
A chicken coop.
I love the youngest one most,
For his scoundrel.
Lying by the waterside,
Shelling seedpods of the lotus.

# Appreciation

This ci-poem titled "Living in a village" is a piece in "A Selected Collection of Flower Hut Ci-poem" written by Xin Qi-ji when he lived in Dai Lake of Shan Yao county, Jiangxi Province. At that time he was not tolerated by the small court, out of work and stayed at home. He styled himself Jia Xuan. The scenery in Dai Lake is very beautiful. There are mountain birds and flowers. The pine trees and bamboos are shooting high to the sky. He got along with the wild old men very well in his prime of life. Leaving the perilous position of official career, he sought for consolation from simple and harmonious idyllic life temporally. Graceful style and fresh village poems were coming down in torrents from his thought. This is one of them.

This ci-poem is an objective imitation of reality. The author kept out of the business, watched in still, took the most poetic scene, and composed this autumn picture of Jiangnan village.

The first part of this ci-poem drew a full view of a peasant family. The thatched eaves were low and small; green grasses were over the stream. The white haired old man and woman speaking in southern accent talked and laughed cheerfully. Happily getting drunk, the author felt flattered by the native sound. Here he describes a simple and indifferent life, self-sufficient. Who were the elderly couple with whitening hair? Perhaps they were the neighbour over the stream. The author seemed to recognize them. Of course, they were common peasants. With a question at the end of the first part, the description became more interesting and charming.

The next part describes the labour life in the countryside. A few words of simple and straight forward style of writings completed a sketch, successfully brought out each different figure in various postures and expressions. In the far side of the picture, the eldest son was hoeing beans. In the near side, the middle one was weaving a chicken coop. By the waterside, the youngest was shelling seedpods of the lotus. These three boy's movement picture had a rich flavour of life, like floating clouds and flowing water—natural and smooth. This ci-poem has a strange ending, excceding all expectations. The poet says the naughty and dishonest youngest son did not work at all, sneaked away, hid in the waterside, had a taste of the new seedpods of the lotus. This is a technique of writing, called " snatching a little leisure from a busy life ". Reading this line we could find that the naughty youngest son's deceiving action, innocent and simple, is really charming.

In this ci-poem there is a stream. The thatched eaves are at the side of it. The eldest son is on the eastern bank. The youngest one is lying by the waterside. The artistic conception is continuous. The stream in Xin Qi-ji's ci-poem ought to be a common shallow water. But it flows happily in readers mind.

# A Short Guide
## to Names of the Tunes
## to Which Ci-poems Are Composed

Ci-pai(詞牌) are names of the tunes to which ci-poems are composed. When people of Tang Dynasty filled a tune, the content and the name of its tune were always unified. Such as the tune of "Fairy Facing the River", always matched a ci-poem talking about fairy's things. "Woman Crown" always said something about Woman Taoist. Since Northern and Southern Song Dynasties, using the old tunes to fill new ci-poems, the contents were always not conformed to the names of their tunes. There were a lot of tunes at that time. Later generations loved the new and loathed the old. Though they filled the old tune, they gave the tune a new name with the meaning of their lines. Thus the same tune always got several different names. Different tunes sometimes got the same names. Such as "Three Platforms" in Tang and Song Dynasty, their names were the same but were different tunes.

In short, where there is a ci-poem; there is a tune. Ci-poem is inseparable from its tune. In this book we gave every ci-poem and the name of its tune free translations and draw the table of each tune above every Chinese ci-poem in order to help readers to understand what ci-poem is. If you have an interest in it, you can use the name of a tune to fill a ci-poem, too. Here we gave brief accounts of names of the tunes. Still for the sake of understanding better.

## 1. Deva-like Barbarian (菩薩蠻)

It was the name of a tune in Jiao Fang of Tang Dynasty (a musical hall in Tang Dynasty later becoming an official brothel). During the years of Tang Xuan Zong (about 850) the state of women barbarian payed tribute to the emperor, they sent a singing and dancing women team whose hair worn in a high bun. They put on golden crown, wore pearls and jewels necklace round their necks. This team was called Deva-like barbarian. Xuan Zong loved singing tunes. The actors took this team's name to creat a tune that was called Deva-like barbarian. Scholars filled this tune too.

There were fourteen such ci-poems of Wen Ting-yun in "A Collection between Flowers". But this legend was not very reliable. One hundred years before Da Zhong (the title of Xuan Zong's reign) there was this tune discovered in a book.

This tune was forty-four characters. The first and second parts each was four lines. Two oblique rhymes changed into two level rhymes. Li Bai's ci-poem was the standarized form.

This tune was also called "Midnight Song" or "A Cloud in the Wu Mountain".

## 2. The Fisherman's Song (渔歌子)

It was the name of a tune of Jiao Fan in Tang Dynasty. Zhang Zhi-he created it. He called himself a mist-covered water fisherman. This ci-poem wrote fisherman's life. Later writers also used this tune to write such lives.

This tune was twenty-seven characters, five lines, four level rhymes.

The other name of this tune was "The Fisherman".

## 3. Song of Teasing (調笑令)

In Tang Dynasty's palace or on their banquet, there was a Pao-Da game. When it was played, a song was singing called teasing Song. This tune was first seen in Wei Yin-wu's ci-poem.

This tune was thirty-two characters, eight lines, four oblique rhymes, two level rhymes, two vowel rhymes. Level and oblique rhymes changed three times. The sixth and seventh lines were two characters' reiterative sentences. They must be the rotated words of the last two words of the fifth line.

After Northern Song, this tune was only used in oblique rhymes.

## 4. *Recalling Jiangnan*（憶江南）

This was a tune created by Li De-yu, (a fellow of Tang Dynasty) for his deceased concubine Xie Qiu-Niang. So it was first called "Xie Qiu Niang". Later Bai Ju-yi changed the name of this tune into "Recalling Jiangnan". Because the first line of his ci-poem was "Jiangnan's wonderful", this tune was also called "Jiangnan's Wonderful", In Jiao Fang of Tang Dynasty, there was a tune called "Dreaming Jiangnan", which was also this tune.

This tune was 27 characters, five lines, three level rhymes.

## 5. *Song of Hourglass at Night*（更漏子）

This tune was first written by Wen Ting-yun of Tang Dynasty. It was forty-six characters. First and second parts were six lines. Two oblique rhymes in the first part were changed into two level rhymes. Three oblique rhymes were changed into two level rhymes in the second part.

The other name fo this tune was "No Hourglass Song".

## 6. *Song of A Woman's Crown*（女冠子）

This was the name of a tune of Jiao Fang in Tang Dynasty.

A woman crown was a woman Taoist. This tune was used to narrate her in poetic form. It was first seen in Wen Ting-yun's ci-poems in "A Collection between Flowers". This tune was forty-one characters, level and oblique rhymes transformed. In the first part there were five lines, twenty-three characters. The first two lines were oblique rhymes, the third and the fifth lines were level rhymes. In the second part there were four lines, eighteen characters. The second and the forth line were level rhymes. This tune was a ditty. There was still a long tune created by Lin Yong, called "A woman Crown Long Song".

## 7. *Call on The Golden Gate*（謁金門）

This was the name of a tune of Jiao Fang in Tang Dynasty. Wei Zhuan's ci-poem of this tune was the standardized form. It was oblique rhymes, forty-five characters. The first part was twenty-one characters, the second part, twenty-four characters. Each part has four lines, four oblique rhymes.

The other names of this tune were "Remembering in Vain" "Flowers Falling by Themselves" etc.

## 8. *Song of Fresh Berries* (生查子)

This was the name of a tune of Jiao Fang in Tang Dynasty. This tune was seen in "A Collection of the Senior". It was oblique rhyme. forty characters. The first and second parts were oblique rhymes, five characters Jue Ju. Every odd number line was no rhyme, but the last character must be level tone. The even number lines rhyme. This tune was first seen in Wei Ying-wu's ci-poems. He Dao's line (a fellow in Song Dynasty) said: "Remember the green silk skirt." So this tune was also called "Green Silk Skirt".

## 9. *Song of the Southern Native Place* (南鄉子)

This was the name of a tune of Jiao Fang in Tang Dynasty. It was twenty-seven characters, two level rhymes, three oblique rhymes. People of Five Dynasties added or decreased some words to form this tune. Hou Shu Ou Yang – Jiong first used this tune.

## 10. *Calming the Disturbance* (定風波)

This was the name of a tune of Jiao Fang in Tang Dynasty. In "A Collection of the Senior", there was this tune. It was first seen in ci-poems of Ou-yang Jiong (a ci-poet in Hou Shu). In this tune the level and oblique rhymes exchanged from one into another. It was sixty-two characters. The first part was five lines, thirty characters, three level rhymes and two oblique rhymes. The second part was six lines, thirty-two characters, four oblique rhymes and two level rhymes. Because the lines were uneven, level rhymes and oblique rhymes interlocked, the tone and temperament were of distinctive features.

The other name of this tune was " Put Down Disturbance Song. "

## 11. *The Beautiful Lady Yu* (虞美人)

This was the name of a tune of Jiao Fang in Tang Dynasty. At first it was used to chant Xiang Yu's (a hero of Qin, called Chu Ba Wan) concubine Yu Ji, so got the name. Later generations used it as a common name of tune.

This tune was fifty-six characters, eight lines. The first and the second parts all were four lines, two oblique rhymes. Then they changed into two level rhymes. The rhymes in these two parts may belong to different vowels.

The other name of this tune was " The Beauty Yu's Song " and " A Full River of Spring Water " etc.

## 12. *Pure Serene Music* (清平樂)

During the time of Kai Yuan (the title of Tang Xuan Zong's reign), the imperial palace grew peonys. They got four varieties: red, purple, pale red and white. The emperor ordered to transplant the flowers to the east of Xin Qin pool, Shen Xiang pavilion. The flowers were in full bloom, The emperor summoned the highest-ranking imperial concubine Yang Gui Fei at moonlit night. The eunuches selected the best actors and sixteen songs. Li Gui-nian (a best singer) intended to organize all the actors to sing. But the emperor said: " With so famous flowers, so beautiful concubine, I don't want old songs. " So Li Bai was called and asked to write three pieces of Pure Serene Music. The actors accompanied with musical instruments. Li Gui-nian sang. Yang Gui Fei poured wine. The emperor blew flute.

" Pure Serene Music " meant music praying for peace and tranquility of the world. Li Bai's four pieces were collected in " A Collection of the Senior ".

This tune was forty-six characters. The first part was four lines, twenty-two characters, oblique rhymes. Every line rhymed. The second part was four lines, twenty-four characters. The rhymes were changed into level. Three lines rhymed.

This tune was also called " Pure Serene Music Song " and " Be drunk in the East Wind " etc.

## 13. *Joy of Meeting* (相見歡)

This was the name of a tune of Jiao Fang in Tang Dynasty. Xue Zhao Yun (a man in Qian Shu) first called this tune " The Joy of Meeting ". LiYu (the emperor of Nan Tang) also used this name of tune. This tune was thirty-six characters, level and oblique rhymes transformed. The first part was three lines, eighteen characters. Every line rhymed level. The second part was four lines, eighteen characters. The first two lines, three words each, rhymed oblique. The last two lines changed into level rhymes. The concluding lines of the first and second parts were all nine characters, they may be upper six lower three or upper four and lower five.

This tune was also called " Crows Crying at Night " (烏夜啼). He Yan's daughter created this tune. He Yan was arrested into prison. His daughter heard crows crying on her roof. She said: " The crying of crows announces good news. My father will be set free. " So she gave the tune this name.

Later " The Joy at Meeting " and " Crows Crying at Night " used the same tune.

The other name of this tune was " Climbing the Western Tower ".

## 14. *Song of Pounding Silk Floss* (搗練子令)

Li Yu chanted pounding silk floss, and created this tune. It was the standard form of Tang ci-poems. Huang Da-yu (a man in Song Dynasty) compiled " Plum Garden ", collected eight pieces of ci-poems of this tune written by anonymous. The beginning line of one of its ci-poems was " Pounding silk floss ". Huang called this tune " Pounding Silk Floss " too, Predecessors often used this tune to write women thinking of their husbands in the army.

This tune was twenty-seven characters, five lines three level rhymes. The other name of this tune was "Pounding Silk Floss".

## 15. *Tipsy in the Land of Peach Blossoms*（醉桃源）

The name of this tune was seen in Li Yu's ci-poem in Southern Tang. It was also called "Lover Ruan Returned"

It is said that during the time of Eastern Han, Liu Chen and Ruan Zhao picked medicines in Tian Tai Mountain. They met two fairy maidens. These two gods urged them to stay for half a year. They longed for returning home very much. When they came back to their native town, the home village was fallen and scattered about. It turned out to be that the time passed in the mountain was seven generations. So this tune got the name and its temperament was very sad.

This tune was level rhyme, forty-seven characters. The first part was four lines, twenty-four characters. Every line rhymed. The second part was five lines, twenty-three characters, four lines rhymed. In the second part, the first two lines, three words each were antitheses.

## 16. *Su Mu Zhe*（蘇幕遮）

This was the name of a tune of Jiao Fang in Tang Dynasty.

Su Mu Zhe originally was dance music of the Western Rigions (a Han Dynasty term for the area west of Yumenguan, including what is now Xinjiang and parts of Central Asia). It was a Transliteration of Gaochan language at that time, which meant a row of people in martial attire, sat on fine horses. The ci-poets of Song Dynasty used this tune to write new songs, which did not have the original meaning. Such as Fan Zhong-yan's ci-poem, Su Mu Zhe.

This tune was sixty-two characters. The first and the second parts were all five lines, four oblique rhymes.

The other name of this tune was "Cloud and Mist Restrain".

## 17. *Bells Ringing in the Continuous Heavy Rain* (雨霖鈴)

This was the name of a tune of Jiao Fang in Tang Dynasty.

According to the < Ming Huan Record > or < Tai Zhen Unauthorized Biography > , the emperor, Tang Min Huan entered Shu to keep clear of An Lu Shan's rebellion. It was raining continuously for ten days. He heard ringing in the plank road. He was mourning for his deceased concubine Yan Gui Fei, so wrote this tune and named it "Bells Ringing in the continuous heavy rain song". The emperor asked an actor Chang Ye-hu to play the instrument. This tune thus handed down. The sound was very sad.

This tune was one hundred and three characters. In the first part there were nine lines, fifty-one characters. The second part, eight lines, fifty-two characters. Each part was five oblique rhymes. The name of this tune was seen in Liu Yong's < A Collection of the Movement > .

It was also called "Bells Ringing in the Continuous Heavy Rain Long Song".

## 18. *Early Youth Wanders* (少年遊)

This tune was seen in "Pearls and Jades Ci-poems" of Yan Shu. One of his line said: "as in the time of early youth permanently", so it got the name.

This tune was fifty characters, ten lines. The first part was five lines, three level rhymes. The second part was five lines, two level rhymes.

This tune was also called "Small Rail".

## 19. *Washing Sand in the Stream* (浣溪沙)

This was the name of a tune of Jiao Fang in Tang Dynasty. The word 'sand' in the name of the tune may change into 'yarn', because Xi Shi (the queen of Wu kingdom) washed yarn in Ro Ye Stream. This tune was also called this name. The tunes can be devided into two types: level rhyme or oblique rhyme. The ci-poem in our book belonged to level rhyme. The tune of level rhyme was forty-two characters. The first part and second part were all three lines. Every line seven words. In the first part, the three lines all rhymed, but the second part, only the second and the third line rhymed. The first two lines antitheses. The syllables of this tune were sprightly. The lines were in good order and were easy to learn by heart, so the ci-poets of graceful and restrained school, or the bold and unconstrained school loved this tune very much.

## 20. *Spring in the Magnificent Pavilion*（玉樓春）

It was the name of a tune of Jiao Fang in Tang Dynasty, and also called " Magnolia "（木蘭花）.

" A Collection between Flowers " reported that " Magnolia " and " Spring in the Magnificent Pavilion " were two different types. But people of Song Dynasty filled " Magnolia " all belonging to " Spring in the Magnificent Pavilion " type.

In " A Collection of the Senior ", Ou-yang Jiong's ci-poem, there was a line which said " Both drunk under the magnolia ", The name of this tune came from it.

This tune was fifty-six characters, eight lines. Each line was seven words. The first part and the second part both were three oblique rhymes.

## 21. *Butterflies Love Flowers*（蝶戀花）

This was the name of a tune of Jiao Fang in Tang Dynasty. Originally it was called " A-Magpie Stepping on a branch. ". Yan Shu used this tune but changed the name into: " Butterflies love Flowers ". This name was taken from the line of Liang Jiang Wen Di (an emperor), which said: " The butterflies turning over on the steps love flowers. " This tune was also first seen in Li Yu's ci-poems (Southern Tang).

It was Sixty Characters, ten lines. The first and second parts all were five lines, four oblique rhymes.

## 22. *Song of Wave Washing Sand* (浪淘沙令)

This was the name of a tune of Jiao Fang in Tang Dynasty. Originally it was a seven characters Jue Ju. In Bai Ju-yi's ci-poem; there was such a line: " Please don't forget Wave Washes Sands ". So it got this name.

" Wave Washes Sand " which was a ditty, two parts, was created by Li Yu (Southern Tang). His ci-poem was the standard form. This tune was level rhyme, fifty-four characters, and ten lines. In the first and second parts the fourth line did not rhyme.

Zhang Song Min (a man in Northern Song) used this tune and changed its name into " The sound of Selling Flowers ".

## 23. *Thinking of Remote One* (思遠人)

This tune was seen in " Xiao Shan (means small mountain) Ci-poems " which was written by Yan Ji-dao (Song dynasty). In his ci-poems, there was a line: " I long for the traveller a thousand li away. " From it this tune got the name.

This tune was nine lines, fifty-one characters, two parts and oblique rhymes.

## 24. *Song of Divination* (卜算子)

This tune was first seen in Su Shi's (A famous writer in Song Dynasty) " Dong Bo Ci-poems ". It was also called " Crescent Moon Hangs on Sparse Paulownia Tree ". The book " Rules of Ci-poems " said the name of this tune took the meaning from " the man of fortune-telling ". Su Shi's ci-poem was the standard form. It was forty-four characters, oblique rhymes. The first and second parts were both four lines. Every even line rhymed oblique. The last words of odd lines should use level tone. Sometimes the two ending lines of each part have Chenzi, that is, word inserted in a line of a ci-poem for balance or euphony. Thus this line was six words.

## 25. *Song of Riverside City* (江城子)

During Tang Dynasty, this tune was only one part. It was first seen in Wei Zhuang's ci-poems. The name of this tune came from Ou-yang Jiong's line: " The mirror of Xi Zi (the Queen of Wu kingdom) illuminates Jiang City. " People of Song Dynasty changed this tune into two parts, seventy characters. The first and second parts were all seven lines, four level rhymes.

This tune was also called " River God Song ".

## 26. *Immortal at the Magpie Bridge* (鵲橋仙)

This tune was first used to chant the Cowherd and the girl Weaver meeting in the seventh evening of the seventh moon on Magpie Bridge. So it got this name. Later people used it as a common name of a tune. It was first seen in Ou-yang Xiu's (A famous writer in Song Dynasty) ci-poems.

It was fifty-six characters, two parts, and ten lines, oblique rhymes. The first and second parts both were five lines, the third and fifth lines rhymed. The ending of each part was seven words, taking upper three, lower four type.

This tune was also called " Meeting During the Time of Jade Dew and Golden Wind Song ".

## 27. *As in a Dream: Song* (如夢令)

Song Su Shi said: " This tune was created by Zhang Zong (king of Later Tang in Five Dynasties). It was first called " Remembering Beautiful Appearance ", only not in good taste. Since there were two reiterative sentences in this ci-poem: " As in a dream, as in a dream, going out to see her off with tears ", the name of this tune was changed into " As in a Dream: Song "

This tune was thirty-three characters, seven lines, five oblique rhymes, and a reiterative rhyme.

It was also called " No Dream Song ".

## 28. *Spring in Peach-blossom Land*（武陵春）

The name of this tune came from Tao Yuan-ming's " The Land of Peach Blossom Notes ", （Tao was a great poet in Jin Dynasty）which recorded the story of a fisherman of Wu Ling entered the land of peach blossom. It was also called " Spring in Men Doing Weapon Practice ".

This tune was level rhyme, two parts, forty-eight characters, and eight lines. The first and second parts both were four lines three level rhymes. Another form was adding a word on the last line.

## 29. *Magnolia Being Reducing in Words*（減字木蘭花）

This tune was also called " Magnolia Stealing Sound ". In order to form this tune, in the first and second part of Magnolia, each first line reduced three words, so got this name. Feng Yan-si of Southern Tang created this tune.

It was two parts, forty-four characters. The first and second parts all were four lines, two oblique rhymes changed into two level rhymes.

## 30. *Telling of Innermost Feeling*（訴衷情）

This was the name of a tune of Jiao Fang in Tang Dynasty. At first it was a tune talking about love affairs. Later it was used to experss one's common emotion. This tune was first seen in " A Collection Between Flowers "

It was forty-four characters. The first part was four lines three level rhymes. The second part was six lines three level rhymes.

## 31. *Song of an Ugly Slave*（醜奴兒近）

This was the name of a tune of Jiao Fang in Tang Dynasty. It was also called " Picking Mulberry Long Song " It was two parts, eighty-nine characters.